Historical American Biographies

HARRY HOUDINI

Escape Artist and Master Magician

Zachary Kent

Enslow Publishers, Inc.

40 Industrial Road   PO Box 38
Box 398   Aldershot
Berkeley Heights, NJ 07922 Hants GU12 6BP
USA   UK

http://www.enslow.com

Library of Congress Cataloging-in-Publication Data

Kent, Zachary.
    Harry Houdini : escape artist and master magician / Zachary Kent.
        p. cm. — (Historical American biographies)
    Summary: Examines the life and career of Harry Houdini, whose
dramatic style, skill at staying in the news, and determination to
continually invent new escapes made him one of the most famous
magicians of all time.
    Includes bibliographical references and index.
    ISBN 0-7660-1619-6
    1. Houdini, Harry, 1874-1926—Juvenile literature. 2. Magicians—
United States—Biography—Juvenile literature. 3. Escape artists—United
States—Biography—Juvenile literature. [1. Houdini, Harry, 1874-1926.
2. Magicians.] I. Title. II. Series.
    GV1545.H8 K48   2003
    793.8'092—dc21
                                            2001008356

10 9 8 7 6 5 4 3

To Our Readers: We have done our best to make sure all Internet Addresses in
this book were active and appropriate when we went to press. However, the
author and the publisher have no control over and assume no liability for the
material available on those Internet sites or on other Web sites they may link to.
Any comments or suggestions can be sent by e-mail to comments@enslow.com or
to the address on the back cover.

Illustration Credits: Reproduced from the Collections of the Library of
Congress, pp. 4, 6, 8, 17, 22, 25, 27, 37, 43, 45, 51, 61, 65, 70, 77, 83,
85, 88, 93, 97, 102, 108, 114.

Cover Illustration: Reproduced from the Collections of the Library of
Congress (Background and Houdini Portrait).

CONTENTS

Harry Houdini

1

SHOWMAN AND MYTHMAKER

Thousands of people crowded along the banks of the Detroit River in Detroit, Michigan. Many more jammed shoulder to shoulder on the Belle Isle Bridge. On November 27, 1906, famed escape artist Harry Houdini prepared to give these spectators an amazing show. He would jump into the river with two sets of handcuffs locked on his wrists. He claimed he could escape from the handcuffs underwater. He believed he could swim back to the surface before he ran out of breath.

"He is smooth-shaven with a keen . . . face, bright blue eyes and thick, curly, black hair," a newspaper reporter described him.[1] He was dressed in his bathing suit, and people noticed his muscled shoulders, arms, and legs. Thirty-three-year-old Houdini exercised constantly to keep himself fit. He would need his strength to escape successfully. A rope was tied around his waist. He could be pulled to safety if he got into too much trouble. But the chance of his drowning still filled the watching crowd with tension. Houdini's assistant, Franz Kukol, stepped forward to give him a final handshake for good luck. Houdini's wife, Bess, hugged him and gave him a kiss.

At last he was ready. He jumped from the bridge. With a splash, he plunged into the chilly water. Everyone's eyes stayed glued to the spot where he had disappeared. They imagined his struggle as he was dragged down deeper and deeper.

Second after second passed. After two minutes, people declared that he was probably drowning. The worry continued to mount, until at last Houdini's

In this picture, Harry Houdini prepares to make a jump into the Charles river in Boston, Massachusetts, in May 1908.

head and shoulders broke the surface of the water. He smiled and waved the opened handcuffs in one of his hands.

That evening, the headlines on the front page of the *The Detroit News* read:

"HANDCUFF KING" JUMPS MANACLED FROM BRIDGE
Handcuff King Houdini Performs Remarkable
Feat and Comes Out Safely
Had a Rope Tied Around his Waist and Tied
to Bridge to Safeguard against Accidents

The article that followed praised Houdini's daring escape:

> Tied by a lifeline a hundred and thirteen feet long, handcuffed with two of the best and latest model handcuffs in the possession of the Detroit police department, nerved by the confidence of a lion in his own powers . . . Houdini, the wonder worker . . . leaped from the draw span of the Belle Isle Bridge at 1 o'clock this afternoon, freed himself from the handcuffs while under water, then swam to a waiting lifeboat, passed over the unlocked and open cuffs and clambered aboard.[2]

Creating a Legend

This bridge jump was good publicity. The stunt would attract people to Detroit's Temple Theatre to see Houdini's show. But he was never satisfied. He wanted his name to become legendary and his life to be unforgettable. In time, he spread a different story of what had happened that day.

Excited spectators watch Houdini drop handcuffed into Boston's Charles River. Bridge jumps such as this one added to Houdini's fame as the world's greatest escape artist.

Houdini's story claimed that he had made his jump in December on a day when the river was frozen. He had leaped from the bridge and through a hole cut in the ice. He freed himself successfully from the handcuffs. But then, while swimming to the surface, he discovered he could not find the hole in the ice. Panic gripped the waiting spectators. Time was running out. Surely Houdini was going to run out of breath. His worried assistant dropped a rope down through the hole. He prayed Houdini would find it and pull himself up. Bess Houdini, too nervous to watch the jump, was waiting in her hotel room. She heard newsboys down in the street shouting, "Houdini drowned! Houdini drowned!"[3]

Trapped beneath the ice, Houdini refused to give up hope. He realized that he could survive by breathing air he found in pockets between the water and the ice. Finally, he saw the dangling rope through the murky water. He grabbed hold of it and pulled himself out. The waiting crowd burst into wild cheers. Back from the hotel, Bess Houdini tearfully clung to him, overjoyed to find him still alive. He had escaped death, and that night he performed at the theater before an excited audience.

That was the thrilling story that Houdini let the public believe. "The secret of showmanship consists not of what you really do," Houdini once explained, "but what the mystery-loving public thinks you do."[4] Harry Houdini believed he was the greatest magician who ever lived. He was a proud man who was determined to succeed. As a magician, Harry Houdini kept many secrets and developed many skills. He became a legend in his own lifetime because he never stopped finding ways to amaze the world.

2

EHRICH WEISS BECOMES HARRY HOUDINI

The city of Budapest, Hungary, had a large Jewish population in the 1800s. Mayer Samuel Weiss was a poor Jewish rabbi in Budapest. His first wife, Rosa Szillag Weiss, died giving birth to a son, Herman, in 1863. A year later, Rabbi Weiss married a second wife, Cecilia Steiner. Although their first child died in 1865, four more Weiss children were born in the years that followed: Nathan in 1868, William in 1870, Ehrich on March 24, 1874, and Theodore in 1876. Rabbi Weiss heard that the United States was a land of golden opportunities. He decided to try to find a better life in America. Leaving his wife and children to wait, Rabbi Weiss made the long journey in 1876.

In 1878, Rabbi Weiss found a good job as the first rabbi in Appleton, Wisconsin. He earned a yearly salary of $750 as Appleton's Jewish religious leader. He saved his money and finally was able to send for his wife and children. In June 1878, Cecilia and the four boys sailed from Hamburg, Germany. The ship plowed through the waves of the Atlantic Ocean and reached New York City after a fifteen-day voyage. The Weiss family lived in a cramped apartment over a store on the main street in Appleton. The family grew even larger when another son, Leopold, was born in 1879.

A Magician in the Family

Rabbi Weiss's first wife was related to a famous Hungarian magician named Compars Herrmann. Herrmann had even performed at the White House for President Abraham Lincoln in 1861. As young Ehrich Weiss grew up, family stories of Compars Herrmann filled him with a special interest in magic.

Ehrich never forgot the first time he attended a traveling circus in Appleton and he saw his first magician. "The man was dressed in a misfitting [sic] dress suit," Ehrich recalled, "[and] had a goatee and mustache."[1] Young Ehrich watched with wonder as this circus magician pulled rabbits out of a top hat and produced coins out of thin air.

In later years, Ehrich Weiss, the boy who would become Harry Houdini, claimed that he first performed in a circus at the age of nine. As part of his act, he said he picked up needles with his eyelashes. In another story, he said he performed as a boy acrobat, calling himself "Eric, Prince of the Air." "Thus, to any young man who has in mind a career similar to mine," he later advised, "I would say: First try bending over backward and picking up a pin with your teeth from the floor, and work up from that into the more difficult exercises."[2] Most likely, however, these stories are untrue.

Hard Times

Many of the Jews in Appleton thought Rabbi Weiss's religious views were too old fashioned. They wanted a rabbi who was open to more modern habits and ideas. In 1882, Rabbi Weiss lost his job. The Weiss family moved to nearby Milwaukee, Wisconsin. There Rabbi Weiss tried to make a living as a teacher of Jewish religion and history. He was unable to find steady work, however. The Weiss family had to move at least five times between 1883 and 1887. "Such hardships and hunger became our lot," Ehrich Weiss unhappily remembered, "that the less said on the subject the better."[3] Gladys, the Weiss's only daughter, was born in Milwaukee in 1882.

At home, the Weisses spoke a German dialect called Yiddish. It was the language they had spoken in Budapest. Growing up, Ehrich learned English while playing with his friends on the streets. His speech was full of slang and bad grammar. He rarely had a chance to attend school. To help support his family, Ehrich started working at a young age. As a newspaper boy, he stood on Milwaukee street corners shouting, "Extra! Extra!" With a tin of polish and a rag, he sometimes earned money as a shoeshine boy. He also delivered telegrams throughout the city as a messenger boy. Any money he earned he brought home to his mother so she could pay the rent and buy food.

More Hard Times

In 1885, Ehrich's half brother Herman died of the lung disease tuberculosis. A little later, on Ehrich's twelfth birthday, Rabbi Weiss took his son aside. The rabbi realized that he had failed to become a success in America. He solemnly asked Ehrich to promise to take care of his mother, as long as she lived.

Ehrich took this promise very seriously. He always had an especially close and loving relationship with his mother. Early the next morning, he ran away from home. He vowed that he would find a good job to provide money for his mother. He sent her a postcard that read: "I am going to [Galveston,] Texas, and will be home in about a year. . . . Your truant son, Ehrich Weiss."[4] He planned to go to Texas, but he mistakenly climbed into a railroad freight car that carried him to Kansas City, Missouri. During the next two years, Ehrich traveled the country looking for work.

At the same time, Rabbi Weiss went to New York City looking for work as a religious teacher. Ehrich eventually made his way to New York, too. He and his father scraped together enough money to rent an apartment on East Seventy-fifth Street. The rest of the family soon traveled from Milwaukee and joined them. "We lived there, I mean starved there, several years," Ehrich grimly remembered.[5]

A Steady Job

In November 1888, fourteen-year-old Ehrich Weiss finally landed a steady job. One day, he noticed a line of young men standing outside H. Richter's Sons, a necktie factory at 502 Broadway. An advertisement board in front of the factory door announced that an assistant necktie cutter was wanted. Ehrich realized he would never get the job if he went to the end of the line. Instead he stepped to the front and boldly announced that the position was filled. Then he entered the factory office, holding the board, and took the job himself.

At about the same time, Ehrich's brother, Theo, got a job with a photographer. The photographer was an amateur magician who one day showed Theo a simple coin trick. When he got home, Theo showed Ehrich the trick. Magic tricks excited Ehrich, and he began to read library books on the subject. He was soon able to do several simple tricks with cards and coins. Another boy at the necktie factory named Jacob Hyman also liked magic. Before long, they put together an amateur magic act, which they performed at parties.

Ehrich and Jacob both enjoyed physical fitness. Together they joined the local Pastime Athletic Club. Ehrich soon won medals in running competitions. He also dove and swam in the dirty waters of the East River, a few blocks away from the Weisses' apartment. Ehrich was determined to build his muscles and live a healthy life. He exercised each morning and vowed never to smoke tobacco or drink alcohol.

The Amazing Robert-Houdin

In 1891, seventeen-year-old Ehrich Weiss bought a book that changed his life. It was the autobiography of Jean-Eugene Robert-Houdin, the great French magician. Robert-Houdin first performed in Paris in

Sixteen-year-old Ehrich Weiss shows off medals he has won in running competitions while a member of the Pastime Athletic Club. As a teenager, Weiss decided he would live a healthy life.

1845, and his autobiography described his amazing show.

From a single wine bottle, Robert-Houdin could pour several different kinds of wines and liquors requested by his audience. Then he magically made an orange tree grow and blossom on the stage. Waving his magic wand, he changed the orange blossoms into bright, round oranges, which he plucked and tossed to audience members. After that, he opened a thin leather briefcase and drew out a cage of birds and two copper pans, one filled with water and the other blazing with fire. His own small son also rose out of the briefcase. Robert-Houdin next blindfolded his son, and the boy was able to describe any object shown by the audience to his father. He identified watches, card cases, and other items in perfect detail. Finally, Robert-Houdin made his son appear to float high above the stage.

After reading Robert-Houdin's book, Ehrich decided he must become a professional magician. "He became my guide and hero . . ." he later declared. "I . . . reread his works until I could recite passage after passage from memory."[6] On April 3, 1891, Ehrich quit his job at the necktie factory. Jacob Hyman also quit and became his partner. They gave magic shows at private parties and performed as a sideshow act in dime museums and on the stage at beer halls. At dime museums, people paid ten cents for a ticket to see entertainment and exhibits.

Ehrich sometimes called himself "Eric the Great" or, when performing card tricks, "Cardo."[7] Finally he settled on the name he would keep. Ehrich mistakenly believed Robert-Houdin's last name was simply Houdin. "When it became necessary for me to take a stage-name," he recalled, "[Jacob Hyman] told me that if I would add the letter 'i' to Houdin's name, it would mean, in the French language 'like Houdin.' I adopted the suggestion with enthusiasm."[8] For years, Ehrich's friends had called him Ehrie, which sounded a lot like Harry. As a magician, therefore, Ehrich Weiss decided to call himself Harry Houdini.

Metamorphosis

He and Jacob Hyman called themselves The Houdini Brothers. They saved their money and purchased an interesting trick. It was a large wooden traveler's trunk with a secret panel that opened inward. The trunk could be locked, but a person could still escape by pulling open the panel. Houdini developed an act with the trunk that he called Metamorphosis, a word of Greek origin meaning "transformation." Onstage, Houdini would climb into a sack inside the open trunk. He invited audience members to tie his hands behind his back. Then he crouched inside the sack, which was then tied and sealed. After that, the trunk was shut and tied with ropes and a screen was drawn around it. Hyman stepped behind the screen, and within seconds Houdini threw open the screen. Houdini stood before the audience, while Hyman had disappeared. When Houdini reopened the trunk, the audience discovered Hyman inside the sack, his hands tied.

The secret of the trick was that while behind the screen, Houdini had released his hands. They had been tied in a manner from which he had learned how to free himself. He slit open the bottom of the sack with a knife and escaped through the trunk's secret panel. Jacob Hyman quickly took his place inside the trunk. By the time the trunk had been untied, unlocked, and reopened, Hyman was inside the sack. No one ever guessed that the bottom of the sack had been cut open. Audiences could not figure out how the switch had been made.

The Columbian Exposition

After four months, Jacob Hyman quit the magic team. He decided instead to perform in show business as a singer and dancer. Houdini needed a new partner, and he asked his brother Theo to join him. In 1893, they traveled to Chicago to take part in the World's Columbian Exposition.

The Columbian Exposition was an international fair. It celebrated the four-hundred-year anniversary of Christopher Columbus's discovery of America in 1492. One of the major attractions of the exposition was an eighty-acre entertainment area called the Midway Plaisance. On the Midway, visitors saw acts from all over the world. The Houdini Brothers performed Metamorphosis twenty times a day. The work earned them twelve dollars a week. It was while performing on the Midway that Houdini first saw a magician escape from a pair of handcuffs. With a handkerchief thrown over his wrists, the magician secretly opened the handcuffs with a hidden key. Houdini studied and practiced the trick until he could perform it perfectly.

Bessie Raymond

The summer of 1894 found the Houdini Brothers performing on the boardwalk at seaside Coney Island, New York. Another boardwalk attraction was an act called "The Floral Sisters, Neat Song and Dance Artists."[9] Theo dated one of the two girls and introduced her to Harry. She was a pretty, brown-haired eighteen year old named Wilhelmina Beatrice Rahmer. She went by the stage name of Bessie Raymond. Twenty-year-old Harry fell in love with her at first sight. In just two weeks, they decided to get married.

Harry and Theo agreed that Bess should replace Theo in the act. It would be easier for a husband and wife to combine their earnings and save on expenses. A local newspaper, the *Coney Island Clipper*, soon printed an announcement that Houdini gave it:

> The brothers Houdini, who for years have mystified the world by their mysterious box mystery, known as Metamorphosis, are no more and the team will hereafter be known as the Houdinis. The new partner is Miss Bessie Raymond . . . who was married to Mr. Harry Houdini on July 22 by Rev. G. S. Louis, of Brooklyn.[10]

It was love at first sight when twenty-year-old Harry Houdini met an eighteen-year-old singer and dancer named Bessie Raymond in the summer of 1894. After just two weeks, they got married.

Bess was Catholic and Harry was Jewish, but their different religions never caused a problem between them. Houdini took his wife home to meet his mother. Rabbi Weiss had died of cancer in 1892. Mrs. Weiss and the rest of the family warmly welcomed Bess. Houdini was especially glad that his dear mother got along with her. "After my coming," Bess recalled, "there were of course two loves in his life, running parallel, so to speak."[11] The two loves Bessie Raymond referred to were herself and Houdini's mother.

Bess soon learned how hard her husband was willing to work to become successful. Houdini rarely slept more than five hours a night. All of his spare time was spent doing physical exercises, practicing rope ties and handcuff magic, and learning coin and card tricks. He taught Bess the part she would play in the act. "It was pleasant," Bess recalled, ". . . to practice tricks with Harry and to [learn] the secrets of his mysteries."[12]

YEARS OF STRUGGLE

The Houdinis
Present their........marvelous mystery
METAMORPHOSIS
Exchange Made in 3 Seconds
The Greatest Novelty Mystery Act in the World![1]

People who saw the Houdinis' poster sometimes became curious enough to pay for a ticket. When the screened cabinet was brought forward to surround the trunk, Bess addressed the audience. "When I clap my hands three times," she declared, "behold a miracle!"[2] She stepped into the cabinet and the audience heard three claps. Instantly Houdini pulled open the curtain. Behind him the trunk remained locked and tied. Bess had disappeared

THE HOUDINIS

PRESENT THEIR

MARVELLOUS MYSTERY

METAMORPHOSIS

→ EXCHANGE MADE IN 3 SECONDS ←

The Greatest Novelty Mystery Act in the World!

All the Apparatus used in this Act is inspected by a Committee selected from the Audience.

Mons. Houdini's hands are fastened behind his back, is securly tied in a bag and the knots are sealed, then placed in a massive box which is locked and strapped, the box is then rolled into a small cabinet, and Mlle. Houdini draws the curtain and claps her hands three times, at the last clap of her hands the curtain is drawn open by Mons. Houdini and Mlle. Houdini has disappeared, and upon the box being opened She is found in his place in the bag, the seals unbroken and her hands tied in precisely the same manner as well Mons. Houdini's when first entering the bag.

Just think over this, the time consumed in making the change is THREE SECONDS,!

We challenge the World to produce an act done with greater Mystery Speed or Dexterity.

Respectfully yours THE HOUDINI'S.

The Houdinis used this handbill to advertise their stage act Metamorphosis in 1895. People who watched the trick were amazed that Harry and Bess could switch places so quickly.

but would soon be revealed inside the trunk. Harry and Bess could make the amazing switch in just three seconds because Bess was smaller and faster than Theo had been.

The couple took what work they could get, mostly in beer halls or dime museums. Bess sang and danced, Harry did coin and card tricks. Together they performed Metamorphosis. Houdini continued to study handcuffs. He bought used handcuffs at pawnshops and took them apart and put them together again, learning how they worked. He discovered that some handcuffs could be opened with a sharp knock between the hinge and the keyhole. Others could be opened with a small piece of metal or bent wire.

The Welsh Brothers' Circus

In April 1895, Harry and Bess joined the Welsh Brothers' Circus, a small traveling tent show that was in Lancaster, Pennsylvania, when they joined it. It was raining the night they arrived in Lancaster. Bess recalled that they "stumbled about through ankle-deep mud for miles in the dark, trying to find the tent."[3] The Welsh Brothers' ten-cent circus featured clowns, acrobats, jugglers, and trained dogs.

The circus went on a tour of small eastern towns. The Houdinis performed Metamorphosis and other magic tricks. Whenever Houdini performed his

Members of the Welsh Brothers' Circus posed for this photograph. Harry and Bess Houdini are seated on the right. The Houdinis performed with the circus when they could find work nowhere else.

handcuff escapes, however, audiences seemed bored. People believed he was using special handcuffs that were easy to open.

Houdini also performed a stunt he called the Needle Trick. He had learned it from a magician at the Columbian Exposition. In this trick, he showed the audience a handful of needles and ten yards of thread. He opened his mouth wide, to prove it was empty. Then he put the needles on his tongue one at a time and seemed to swallow them. After that, he gulped down the length of thread and opened his mouth to show that it was still empty. Reaching between his lips, he began pulling out the thread. Bess held the end, as Houdini slowly stepped backward. Strung upon the thread were all of the needles shining in the stage lights. The audience was amazed.

The American Gaiety Girls

The Houdinis always mailed half of their weekly twenty-dollar salary home to Harry's mother. When the circus season ended, he and Bess still had enough savings to invest in a run-down traveling variety show. It was called the American Gaiety Girls. In the autumn of 1895, the Houdinis joined

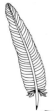

Circus Wild Man

A poster at the Welsh Brothers' Circus advertised a "wild man," although no one in the company was assigned to play that role. One night, however, the audience demanded to see the untamed creature. Circus owner John Welsh yelled to Harry: "Hey, kid . . . throw some paint on your face. . . . We gotta have a wild man."[4] Houdini quickly created a costume from burlap sacks. He smeared grease paint on his face and climbed into a cage that was rolled in before the audience. Houdini howled and gnawed on a piece of raw meat to the delight of the crowd. His successful wild man act became a regular part of the circus show.

the American Gaiety Girls on a tour of eastern towns.

During this tour, Houdini came up with the idea of visiting police stations and challenging the police to lock him into handcuffs. The police in Holyoke, Massachusetts, handcuffed him. They were surprised when he escaped in less than a minute. He did the same escape in other towns, but local newspaper stories failed to gain him the publicity he wanted. The Houdinis were unable to make their traveling show a success. In the spring of 1896, the American Gaiety Girls went out of business.

The Straitjacket Escape

Out of work once again, the Houdinis signed up with Marco the Magician for a tour of eastern Canada. Marco was the stage name of Edward J. Dooley. Dooley was an amateur magician from Connecticut who dreamed of becoming famous. The show traveled to the province of Nova Scotia. But audiences did not think much of it. Unable to pay the Houdinis, Marco simply quit and handed over the show to them.

While performing in St. John, New Brunswick, Houdini one day visited the local lunatic asylum. As the director showed him around, they stopped outside a padded cell. Through a small, barred window, Houdini saw a violent patient struggling to get out of a straitjacket. Houdini had never seen a straitjacket before. He could not get the dramatic image of the struggling patient out of his mind. The next day he returned to the asylum and persuaded the director to give him an old straitjacket. He returned to his hotel room, determined to learn how to escape from it. Bess strapped him into the canvas jacket, and for hours he rolled about the floor, trying to free himself. Bess finally released him, but the next day he insisted on trying again.

Each day for a week he grappled with the challenge. He groaned with exhaustion and constant straining, but one day at last he was able to bring his wrapped arms to the front of his body. He managed to open the buckles of the leather sleeve straps with his teeth. Pressing through the canvas material with his aching fingers, twisting his body, and thrashing on the floor, he finally learned how to free himself.

Houdini tried performing the straitjacket escape in his show. He released himself after straining behind the curtains of his cabinet. When he proudly stepped out free at last, his clothes were rumpled and his body was sweating. But the crowd was not impressed. People muttered that somebody probably had snuck inside the cabinet and unbuckled him.

Magic Teacher

Harry and Bess returned home to New York City without a penny in their pockets. Houdini had spent five years as a professional magician, yet he was still a failure. Worried about his future, he set up Professor Harry Houdini's School of Magic. "DO YOU WANT TO LEARN AN ACT?" asked his advertisement. "If you want to go on the Stage, travel with a Circus, play Variety theatres or Museums, you must first learn to do something to attract Attention."[5] He offered to teach magic and sell tricks by mail.

However, that effort was even a failure, and in the autumn of 1897, he returned to performing. He and Bess took their magic act back on the road. They traveled from city to city, accepting whatever jobs and wages they could find.

The California Concert Company

In December 1897, the Houdinis joined the California Concert Company at a salary of twenty-five dollars a week. It was a traveling medicine show, run by Thomas Hill. Each day, the show rolled into a small town in a large open carriage. One member of the show would play an organ. Houdini tapped a tambourine, Bess sang, and soon people would gather. When the crowd was big enough, Hill loudly described his wonderful, cure-all medicine, which he then sold by the bottle. Each evening in the town's hall, the company gave a full show. The evening show included a play, music, and the Houdinis' magic, as well as the selling of more of Hill's medicine.

On one occasion, Hill suggested that the Houdinis pretend to be spirit mediums to help the show. Spirit mediums claimed they could reveal messages from the dead. Houdini quickly gathered personal information that he could reveal to the audience that night. "I had gone around to the cemeteries and read all of the inscriptions on tombstones, looked over a few birth and death records and acquired a lot of information from the gossips," he recalled. "I was ready to answer almost anything."[6] The act was a success, but Houdini did not enjoy tricking people this way.

The Handcuff Challenge

In April 1898, the Houdinis rejoined the Welsh Brothers' Circus for another six months. As part of their act, Houdini tried performing his Straitjacket Escape and his Handcuff Escape. But audiences showed little interest in these tricks.

Late in the year, Kohl & Middleton's Dime Museum in Chicago, Illinois, invited the Houdinis to perform for a few weeks. Houdini persuaded the theater manager to introduce him to some Chicago newspaper reporters. He bragged to the reporters that he could escape from the city jail after being handcuffed and locked in a cell. Police Lieutenant Andy Rohan thought it would be amusing to hear Houdini calling for help from within a cell. He agreed to lock him up and let him struggle. Surprisingly, within a minute, Houdini returned to Rohan's office completely free.

The reporters, however, did not think much of his escape. They had learned that Houdini had visited the jail a few times. They guessed he had examined the locks and had made keys he could secretly use. Houdini quickly responded, "Okay, if you think I'm using some cheap trickery . . . strip me stark naked and search me. Get a doctor to search me. Then lock me up again."[7] They agreed and left him handcuffed naked in a cell. In just ten minutes, he escaped both the handcuffs and the cell and was back in Rohan's office, dressed in his clothes.

Houdini's jail escape made news in the January 5, 1899, issue of the *Chicago Journal*. The publicity brought huge audiences to Kohl & Middleton's Dime Museum to see him escape from handcuffs and leg irons on stage. Houdini quickly sent clippings of the newspaper story to several Chicago theater managers. As a result, the Hopkins Theater, Chicago's top variety theater, hired him for a couple of weeks.

Martin Beck

Early 1899 found the Houdinis performing their act in a beer hall in St. Paul, Minnesota. One evening after the show, a man named Martin Beck introduced himself. Beck hired acts for the Orpheum circuit. The Orpheum circuit was the most important chain of variety theaters in the West, stretching from Chicago to San Francisco.

Beck had a definite opinion about the Houdinis' act. He liked Metamorphosis and the Challenge Handcuff Escape. He thought, however, that Houdini's card tricks, coin tricks, and other magic were uninteresting. Beck advised Houdini to specialize in escapes. This was unexpected advice, but Houdini agreed to give it a try.

In April, Beck hired the Houdinis to perform at the Orpheum Theater in Omaha, Nebraska, for sixty dollars a week. For publicity, Houdini escaped from five pairs of police handcuffs and a set of leg irons at the city police department. "MANACLES DO NOT HOLD HIM," exclaimed the *Omaha World-Herald*. "The entire handcuffs and leg irons of the police department were on exhibition and all of them were used that could be worn conveniently . . ."[8]

Escape Secrets

After Omaha, Beck gave the Houdinis a raise to ninety dollars a week. He sent them off to begin a

Letter of Proof

Every time Houdini escaped from handcuffs at a police station, he asked for a signed document to prove what he had done. The chief of police in Memphis, Tennessee, wrote the following letter of proof on October 24, 1899:

To whom it may concern: This is to certify that Mr. Harry Houdini gave an exhibition at the Central Police Station in this city to-day in the presence of about twenty-five officers, and we can highly endorse him as a wonder in his line. We placed seven pairs of handcuffs on him at one time and in every manner possible, and he released himself in less than ten minutes. He was previously stripped naked and searched. Jerome E. Richards, Chief of Police.[9]

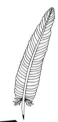

tour of West Coast Orpheum theaters. In San Francisco, on July 13, 1899, Houdini entered the police station and made his handcuff challenge. He stripped off his clothes and a doctor examined him. No keys or pieces of wire or metal were found hidden in his mouth, in his ears, or anywhere else on his body. The doctor looked at his armpits, between his toes, and even ran a comb through his wavy hair.

It is uncertain where Houdini hid the small tools he needed to pick locks. But other magicians have offered suggestions. After his hands were examined, Houdini might have distracted the doctor with a comment or movement. In a split second, he could then recover some tiny tool stuck somewhere on his body with a piece of wax. He could keep the tool hidden in his hand because it already had been searched. A lock-picking tool, such a short piece of thin wire, sometimes could in fact be hidden in his thick hair. In addition, many men, especially doctors, wore black suits in those days. It is thought that Houdini might have sometimes prepared a tiny black cloth bag with his tools inside. With a little wire hook, he could have skillfully attached the bag, unnoticed, to the doctor's back, then secretly snatched it back after the examination. It has also been guessed that Houdini sometimes hid a small wire in the thick skin on the sole of a foot. That was a location a doctor would be likely to miss. Houdini could have used any of these methods to aid him in his escapes.[10]

When making jail escapes, Houdini usually examined the cell before allowing himself to be locked inside. He could hide a piece of wire or a small key in a crack in the floor or within reach outside the cell door. Houdini also developed other talents. Years of practice made him very skillful with his hands. Even though he was handcuffed, his fingers could reach the keyholes. He once revealed, "The [first] lesson is to learn to use both hands. . . . when at [the dinner] table I practiced to use the left hand [constantly], until I could use it almost as

easily as the right."[11] He also did exercises with his bare feet. He became so skilled that he could thread a needle with his toes.

The King of Handcuffs

Houdini had now mastered most common handcuffs. His escape act became a great success. Bess performed only as his assistant now. They were no longer advertised as "The Houdinis." He now called himself "Houdini: The King of Handcuffs."[12]

Houdini attracted attention because the sheer suspense and surprise of his escapes held his audiences spellbound. Before long, Beck raised his salary to one hundred fifty dollars a week. This was at a time when the average American factory worker earned only about ten dollars a week.

The Orpheum tour ended in the autumn of

Harry Houdini, the King of Handcuffs, had learned, after years of practice, how to escape from handcuffs in record time.

1899. Houdini was quickly hired by the Keith circuit, the leading theater chain in the East. Among other cities, he played Boston and New York. But when the tour ended in February, he found himself once again out of work. Houdini was not discouraged. If he could not find work in the United States, he would look for it somewhere else. He soon told Bess, "Pack your bags. We're going to London."[13]

4

TRIUMPH IN EUROPE

Houdini decided to try his luck in Europe, even though he had no contacts there. On May 30, 1900, he and Bess boarded a ship bound for England. Throughout the long Atlantic Ocean voyage, Houdini suffered terribly from seasickness. The rolling of the ship on the waves sometimes sickened him so much that he claimed he wanted to kill himself. Bess finally tied him to his bunk to keep him from jumping overboard.

The Scotland Yard Escape

At last the couple arrived in London, England, and Houdini began his search for work. He showed theater managers his newspaper clippings and police certificates. But he was unable to attract much interest. Then he met a young theatrical agent named Harry Day. Day approached C. Dundas Slater, manager of the Alhambra, a famous London variety theater. Slater refused to believe Houdini's claim that he could escape from any handcuffs. "Go down to Scotland Yard," he challenged, "and if you can get out of their handcuffs I might give you a try."[1] Scotland Yard was the headquarters of the London police department.

Houdini jumped at this chance to show his skills. Before sailing for England, he had mastered all eight types of British handcuffs. On June 14, 1900, Houdini arrived with Slater at Scotland Yard. The police superintendent at Scotland Yard also scoffed at Houdini's claims. To test him, he took a pair of police handcuffs and locked Houdini's arms around a pillar. "Here," he jokingly announced, "is the way we handle Yankees who come over here and get into trouble." He turned to Slater with a smile. "Let's leave him here for a time," he suggested. "We'll come back in an hour." Before the superintendent and Slater reached the door, Houdini called out to them, "If you're going back to the office, I'll go with you."[2] They turned with surprise to see Houdini walking toward them with the opened handcuffs in his hand.

The Bean Giant

The Scotland Yard escape won Houdini a great deal of publicity. Just three weeks after arriving unknown in England, he opened at the Alhambra. On his opening night, a man in the audience suddenly interrupted his act. He was a magician who called himself The Great Cirnoc. He insisted that he was the original Handcuff King, not Houdini.

In response, Houdini showed the audience a special pair of handcuffs. They were known as the Bean Giant, invented by Captain Charles Bean of Boston, Massachusetts. The tiny keyhole of these handcuffs seemed beyond the reach of the fingers of the person locked in them. Houdini challenged Cirnoc to escape from the Bean Giant to prove his greatness. Cirnoc promised that he would make the escape if Houdini did so first. Calmly, Houdini allowed Cirnoc to lock the cuffs on him. He entered his screened cabinet and after a few seconds in hiding stepped out again with his hands free. Now it was Cirnoc's turn. Houdini locked the handcuffs on him, but try as Cirnoc might, he could not escape from them. Houdini finally had to release him. Admitting defeat, Cirnoc shook Houdini warmly by the hand. The audience wildly cheered Houdini as the greater of the two magicians.

For many weeks, Houdini performed before sell-out crowds. Each evening, people brought handcuffs to challenge him, and Houdini always successfully escaped from them. *The Showman* magazine called Houdini "Probably the most mysterious and wonderful entertainer the world has ever seen."[3] He could have stayed in England much longer, but Harry Day had arranged for him to perform in Germany next.

On to Germany

The Houdinis traveled to Dresden, Germany, in September 1900. As always, Houdini quickly gained publicity by escaping from handcuffs at police headquarters. It was the custom of German audiences to whistle if they did not like an act. Gustave Kammsetzer, manager of the Central Theatre, gave Houdini a warning. If the audience whistled on his opening night, Kammsetzer would be forced to cancel their contract.

Houdini began to win audience approval the moment he stepped onstage and spoke to them in German. Then he quickly escaped from handcuffs and leg irons borrowed from the Mathildegasse Prison. The locks on the leg irons alone weighed forty pounds. Instead of whistling, the audience jumped to its feet and cheered after his surprising escape. "When that audience rose in a solid mass . . .," Houdini recalled, "I knew I was going to stay my full engagement."[4]

In October, Houdini performed at the Wintergarten Theater in Berlin. He first escaped naked from handcuffs and leg irons at the Berlin police headquarters. News of his escape brought people crowding to the Wintergarten ticket office hoping to see Houdini's wonderful escapes onstage.

During his month in Berlin, Houdini spent daytime hours at the shop of a locksmith named Mueller. He volunteered to work there because it gave him a chance to study German locks. "Mueller . . . was more than willing that I should work for nothing," Houdini remembered, "and I commenced repairing locks for him. He soon discovered that his 35 years of experience was nothing as compared to my trick in opening locks."[5]

Houdini's handcuff escapes were an instant success in Europe. German audiences were also charmed when he spoke German to them.

Continued Success

Twenty-seven-year-old Houdini had become such a sensation that rival magicians began to imitate him with handcuff acts all over Germany. Houdini was determined to take full advantage of the popular trend. He sent a telegram to his brother, Theo, in New York: "COME OVER THE APPLES ARE RIPE."[6] By this he meant that the European audience loved magic and that Theo should come over and take advantage of it. Theo was performing magic in the United States using the stage name "Hardeen." Houdini arranged for Theo to perform in German towns he himself did not have time to visit. When Theo arrived in Germany, Houdini was overjoyed to learn that he had brought their mother with him.

It was Theo who discovered how to make the Straitjacket Escape successful. When the trick was done behind a screen, there was nothing to prove that he had not gotten help. One night after the audience grumbled loudly, Theo promised to repeat the escape in full view. Two nights later, a sellout crowd cheered wildly after watching him escape before their eyes. Theo sent Houdini copies of the newspaper stories. Impressed, Houdini began performing the Straitjacket Escape in front of audiences, too. After witnessing his performance, one reporter exclaimed, "He wriggles and squirms . . . slips his head under his arm, skates along on one shoulder, chews a buckle or two, and peels off his crazy house trappings as a boy does his bathing suit."[7] Houdini traveled through England, France, and Germany in 1901 and 1902. He thrilled audiences with the Straitjacket Escape everywhere he went.

The Russian Carette

In the spring of 1903, Houdini hired an assistant, an Austrian named Franz Kukol, to help him perform his escapes. Onstage, Kukol was often able to distract audiences by pretending to be clumsy. Houdini admitted, "We want you to get the idea that [our

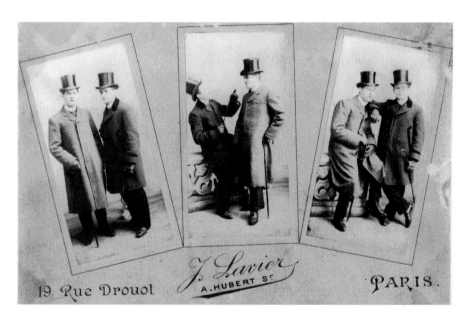

Houdini (the shorter man in the dark jacket) poses in photographs with his brother, Theo, in 1901. Theo performed escapes under the name "Hardeen."

assistants] play no real part in the performance of our tricks; whereas, of course, they are most important."[8]

That May, Houdini agreed to perform in Russia. In the streets of Moscow, he saw strange vehicles called carettes. Heavily locked and bolted, these horse-drawn cells were used to carry prisoners eastward to Siberia. Houdini approached the chief of the Moscow police and asked for permission to escape from one. "No one has ever escaped from the carette," the officer sternly responded.[9] Still, he agreed to give Houdini the chance.

On May 11, Houdini was stripped naked and thoroughly searched. Then he was led into a carette with his wrists and ankles bound in irons. Only after

Queen Victoria's Gown

Great Britain's Queen Victoria died on January 22, 1901. In London, a dress shop respectfully displayed a gown it had designed for the queen. When Houdini saw it, he marveled at the fact that Queen Victoria and his mother must have been the same size. He persuaded the shop to sell the gown to him. After performing in Germany, he took his mother to Budapest, Hungary. She had not been back since leaving in 1878. At the city's best hotel, Houdini insisted his mother dress in the gown designed for Queen Victoria. It gave him great pleasure to see her greet visiting friends and relatives looking like a queen.

being locked inside was he told that the only key to open the carette door was thousands of miles away in Siberia. If he failed to escape, he faced a long, cold journey. Fearless, Houdini managed to free himself in less than an hour. Some magicians believe that while giving Houdini a good-luck kiss, Bess passed from her mouth to his the small escape tool he needed.

Houdini performed in Russia until September 1903 and was a huge success. During a single week in Moscow he earned the sum of $1,750. He wrote to a friend, "Things are still booming with us, and we have never been in such demand as at the present moment."[10]

The *Mirror* Newspaper Challenge

Houdini returned to England in November 1903, recognized as one of Europe's leading entertainers. Birmingham locksmith Nathaniel Hart had spent five years inventing a set of handcuffs. Hart claimed no one could open them. A London newspaper, *The Daily Illustrated Mirror*, bought the handcuffs and challenged Houdini to escape from them. Houdini accepted the challenge.

On March 17, 1904, an audience of four thousand crowded into the London Hippodrome. A reporter from the *Mirror* clapped the handcuffs on Houdini's wrists. Then he turned the key six times to lock the bolt. Houdini announced from the stage, "I am now locked up in a handcuff that has taken a British mechanic five years to make. I do not know whether I am going to get out of it or not, but I can assure you I am going to do my best."[11]

Houdini stepped behind the screen of his cabinet, while the theater orchestra began to play. Minute after minute ticked by, while the orchestra played on. After twenty minutes, Houdini stuck his head out of the cabinet. He was still handcuffed. He explained that he needed to get a better look at the lock in the bright stage lights. The orchestra played a waltz as Houdini ducked back inside the cabinet. After another fifteen minutes, he came out again. The handcuffs remained locked firmly on his wrists. This time he requested a cushion because his knees had begun to hurt inside the cramped cabinet. A cushion was handed to him. Another twenty minutes passed, and again Houdini appeared, still handcuffed. The audience groaned with disappointment. It seemed that Houdini was now exhausted from his efforts to escape. He asked the reporter from *The Daily Illustrated Mirror*, "Will you remove the handcuffs for a moment, in order that I may take my coat off?"[12]

The reporter refused. He believed that if Houdini saw how the handcuffs were unlocked, it would be too helpful. So with difficulty Houdini pulled a penknife from his vest pocket. He yanked open the blade with his teeth. Then he drew his coat over his head and calmly cut it to pieces. The audience cheered as Houdini threw off the cut pieces and went back inside the cabinet.

Houdini had been handcuffed for one hour. But the audience had never grown bored. With each passing minute, the feeling of suspense increased. Ten minutes slowly ticked by. "The band was just finishing a stirring march," exclaimed the article published later in the *Mirror*,

> when, with a great shout of victory, Houdini bounded from the cabinet holding the shining handcuffs in his hand—free! A mighty roar of gladness went up. Men waved their hats, shook hands one with the other. Ladies waved their handkerchiefs, and [audience members,] rushing forward as one man, shouldered Houdini, and [carried] him in triumph around the arena.[13]

Houdini seemed overcome with emotion, and he sobbed openly.

According to one story, this was not the great success it appeared to be. After struggling for an hour, Houdini had called Bess to him and whispered that he was in serious trouble. If he could not get the handcuff key, he would be forced to admit he was beaten. Bess, it was rumored, went to the newspaper reporter and tearfully begged him for help. Her husband's future as a performer would be ruined if he failed. She won the reporter's sympathy. He gave her the key, and she smuggled it to Houdini in a glass of water.[14]

A Visit Home

At the end of May 1904, the Houdinis returned to the United States for three months to visit Harry's mother. In New York City he bought a large brownstone house at 278 West 113th Street. He planned to live there with his wife and mother. It stood four stories high and contained twenty-six rooms. The Houdinis had no children, but they would still need every bit of space. Houdini had begun a lifelong hobby of collecting thousands of books on magic, witchcraft, spiritualism, and related subjects. As the years passed, magic books, magazines, theater playbills, and theater posters would fill many of the rooms.

Books began to pile up everywhere. A visitor to the house later recalled, "They lined the walls on all sides, pressing against one another for elbow-room and well-nigh touching the ceiling."[15] Houdini enjoyed collecting unusual things. He owned letters written by famous people, including almost all of the signers of the Declaration of Independence. He also owned religious leader Martin Luther's Bible, author Edgar Allan Poe's writing desk, and the first electric chair.

Houdini had this picture taken with the two women he loved the best, his mother, Cecilia Weiss, and his wife, Bess. In 1904, he bought a house in New York City where they all could live together.

The Packing Crate Challenge

In August 1904, the Houdinis sailed back to Great Britain. Houdini was earning as much as two thousand dollars a week now. In September, in Glasgow, Scotland, he introduced a new trick. In the lobby of the theater where he was performing, he put a packing crate on display, so people could closely examine it. It looked solidly built. It was believed that if Houdini was nailed inside, he would be unable to escape. The night before his opening performance, however, Houdini and Franz Kukol snuck into the empty theater. They yanked out the long nails from one of the crate's side panels. They clipped them short and nailed them back in place. Now Houdini was ready to give his show.

"The Northern District of the city was in a state of uproar last night," the *Glasgow Herald* reported excitedly on September 22,

> . . . You might have walked on the heads of the surging, struggling, swaying mass of people. . . . And yet the explanation was simple. Houdini, the Handcuff King and Prison Breaker, was announced to have accepted a most unique challenge. . . . He . . . meant to get out of the box. . . . specially made in order to test his ability. . . .[16]

A committee from the theater audience nailed Houdini inside the crate. Then his screened cabinet was placed around it. Hidden from view, Houdini quickly pushed open the panel with the short nails and got out easily. He pushed the panel back in place, then waited several minutes to let the suspense build in the audience. At last, he revealed himself to wild applause.

A few rival magicians soon figured out how he did this trick. They began performing the escape using coffins instead of packing crates. Houdini found a way to embarrass them. On September 30, he had a coffin brought onstage and showed how the magicians substituted short screws in order to escape. Then he replaced the short screws with long screws. He climbed into the coffin and had the lid closed and sealed. Hidden within his cabinet, Houdini amazed the audience by escaping in just a few minutes. Yet the coffin remained apparently untouched.

People did not realize that the long screws in the bottom of the coffin were inserted into wooden dowels. The wooden dowels themselves could be slipped secretly in and out of holes. Houdini had escaped by using his strength to separate the entire coffin from its bottom. While the theater orchestra played loudly to cover the noise, he pounded the coffin back together. The wooden dowels fit perfectly into the coffin's sides.

By 1905, Houdini had spent four and a half years in Europe. He had made himself an astonishing success. But he yearned for even greater fame.

5

CONQUERING NEW CHALLENGES

HOUDINI

The Marvel of the Age
The Wizard of the Chains
The Demon of the Cells
The Mystic of the World
NOTHING CAN HOLD HIM! NOTHING![1]

A 1905 advertisement made these claims, and most people who saw Houdini's act agreed. His fame as an escape artist had spread throughout Europe. Now he felt he was ready to conquer the United States. He returned to New York City and opened at the Colonial Theater on October 2, 1905. He followed with performances in Detroit,

Cleveland, Rochester, and Buffalo. Everywhere he went, audiences packed the theaters to see him.

The Assassin's Cell Escape

In Washington, D.C., on January 6, 1906, Houdini made news with a fantastic prison escape. At the tenth precinct jail, he visited "murderers' row," seventeen cells, just then containing nine dangerous prisoners. Cell no. 2 had been the cell of Charles Guiteau, the man who had assassinated President James Garfield in 1881. A man named Hamilton, on trial for murdering his wife, currently occupied the cell.

Houdini had himself locked naked inside cell no. 2 while Hamilton stared in confusion. From whatever hiding places he had chosen, in his hair, between his toes, or somewhere else within reach, Houdini produced the pieces of wire he used to pick locks. He freed himself without difficulty. Then, still naked, he quickly ran along the row of cells, unlocking each one. He told the prisoners to switch cells, and then he locked them up again. "As I was stripped . . .," Houdini later recalled, "the prisoners thought the devil, or someone [like] him, was in their presence, and, trembling with fear, they obeyed my command."[2] Swiftly he dressed and surprised the prison warden and gathered newspaper reporters with his escape. Altogether, the amazing stunt had taken less than twenty-seven minutes.

While on tour in 1906, Houdini escaped from a number of jail cells. It was wonderful publicity for his stage show. Often, his assistant, Franz Kukol, prepared the way by secretly examining the lock of the cell door. Then, later, Kukol could drop the necessary key or tool outside the cell, hidden in a bit of scrap paper. With chewing gum stuck on the bottom of his bare foot, Houdini could pick it up on his way into the cell.[3]

Creating a Legend

Naked jail escapes were just one method Houdini used to get publicity. No entertainer in the world did more to keep his name before the public. Houdini often made up stories to make himself seem more interesting. "When I was a youngster . . . my mother took me out and apprenticed me to a locksmith," Houdini told the *Washington Times* in 1906, for example. "That is where I got my first knowledge of the weakness of locks. I discovered a method of opening them which I kept to myself."[4] The story has never been proven to be true.

In 1906, Houdini published his first book, *The Right Way to Do Wrong*. The ninety-six-page pamphlet revealed many of the tricks used by con men, thieves, and pickpockets. It was sold in the theater lobby wherever Houdini performed. That same year, Houdini began publishing *The Conjurer's Monthly* magazine. Filled with news of interest to magicians, the ten-cent magazine appeared until August 1908.

Between 1906 and 1908, Houdini toured the United States. He dreamed up a series of curious challenge escapes to keep people amazed. In Philadelphia, a college football team carried a giant leather football into the theater. They locked Houdini in chains inside the ball. Then they laced the ball closed with another set of chains and a huge padlock. Houdini escaped in thirty-five minutes. Onstage in Boston, six boilermakers sealed Houdini inside an iron boiler using red-hot rivets. Houdini escaped in less than an hour. In Los Angeles, he somehow got out of a locked canvas U.S. government mailbag. And each time he made an escape, he left the container locked or undamaged. Rumors that Houdini had supernatural powers soon began to spread.

Jumping From Bridges

On November 27, 1906, Houdini made his first fantastic bridge jump from the Belle Isle Bridge in Detroit, Michigan. Successfully, he freed himself from handcuffs under water. In May 1907, he leaped in handcuffs and leg irons from a bridge in

Generous Houdini

Houdini rarely had any savings because he spent so much money adding to his book collection. He was also a very generous man. In Glasgow, Scotland, in 1904, for example, he gave away four hundred pairs of shoes to barefoot children. Anyone with a hard luck story could depend on getting help from him. He made regular gifts of money to several old magicians. He could not keep track of all the money he gave away. One day a man joyfully stepped up to greet him. Houdini claimed he did not know the man. "But you have been paying my rent for the past eleven years!" the man insisted.[5]

Rochester, New York. Two weeks later, forty thousand people watched him jump from the Seventh Street Bridge in Pittsburgh, Pennsylvania. To increase the suspense of his jumps, he learned how to stay underwater longer. He practiced at home in his bathtub. In time, he could hold his breath underwater for more than three minutes. He also learned to endure cold so he could jump in winter weather. He floated chunks of ice in his bathwater and dunked himself, holding his breath.

Despite all of his stunts, Houdini discovered he was growing less popular. So many magicians copied him that his escapes began to seem common. In January 1908, while performing in St. Louis, Missouri, Houdini wrote in his diary, "Manager Tate informs me, 'You are not worth a five-dollar bill to me.' I told him, 'I hope you are mistaken.' We shall see."[6] It seemed clear that Houdini needed a stunning new trick if he wanted to keep attracting audiences.

The Water Can Escape

Houdini thought very carefully and invented something new. In January 1908, he first performed the Water Can Escape at the Columbia Theater in St. Louis. First, Houdini's assistants spread a sheet of canvas across the floor of the stage. Then they brought out a large iron can with a lid that could be locked by six padlocks. It stood forty-two inches high and was shaped like a dairy milk can. But it was large enough to hold a man.

Houdini invited several audience members onto the stage to inspect the can. While he left the stage to change into a bathing suit, the can was filled with twenty-two pails of water. When he returned, he announced that he would demonstrate how long he could remain underwater. He challenged the audience to try to hold its breath as long as he could. Most people were gasping before two minutes had passed. Yet it was a full three minutes before Houdini surfaced.

Having made his point, Houdini allowed himself to be handcuffed. He sank under the water in the can. The lid was screwed on and locked with six padlocks. Franz Kukol pulled the curtained cabinet around the can to hide it. The orchestra played the song "Many Brave Hearts Lie Asleep in the Deep," and the audience waited.

People kept careful track of the time. They knew Houdini could stay underwater a long time. But after two minutes they began to worry. The suspense increased with each passing second. At three minutes, it seemed Houdini surely must be in trouble. Time continued to pass, one long second after another. The tension seemed unbearable when suddenly Houdini, soaking wet, threw back the curtain and stepped out of the cabinet. With a sweep of his arm, he revealed that behind him the can remained locked. This was something startling and new. Houdini's Water Can Escape thrilled audiences wherever he performed it.

The secret of the escape was simple. The top third of the can was attached to the rest only by two trick rivets. While inside the can, Houdini unscrewed the rivets, pushed open the top, and climbed out—without ever touching the padlocks. There were also tiny airholes located in the lid to make sure he would never suffocate, no matter how long he took.[7]

The new act created a sensation. All the magicians doing handcuff escapes could not equal it. In

In this publicity photo, Houdini is about to be padlocked inside his specially built water can. Although escape looked impossible, the trick was really quite simple.

the spring of 1908, Houdini performed throughout the United States. Each evening he began his act with the Straitjacket Escape. The audience marveled at the energy and strength he used to get free. Next he did Metamorphosis, assisted by Bess; then he did the Needle Trick. But it was the Water Can Escape that he always used as the stunning finish to his act.

Return to Europe

On August 10, 1909, Houdini and Bess sailed again to Europe. While in England, he hired master mechanic and woodworker James Collins to join his team. He also hired a third assistant, James Vickery, to handle general duties. Houdini insisted that anyone who worked for him sign an oath: "I the undersigned do solemnly swear on my sacred honor . . . that as long as I live I shall never [reveal] the secret or secrets of Harry Houdini, or any thing I may make for him and the secret of the can. I further swear never to betray Houdini. . . . "[8]

Houdini began his European tour at the Circus Busch, in Berlin, Germany. He performed at the Hansa Theater in Hamburg in November 1909. While in Hamburg, Houdini saw his first airplane during a flying demonstration at a local racetrack. It had been only six years since inventors Orville and Wilbur Wright made the first successful airplane flight at Kitty Hawk, North Carolina. Houdini watched in awe as German pilot Hans Grade flew a double-winged biplane over the racetrack. When the plane returned to earth, Houdini excitedly rushed across the field. He asked Grade where he could buy a plane. Within a week, Houdini had bought a new French Voisin biplane for five thousand dollars. He also hired a Voisin company mechanic named Antonio Brassac. Brassac would keep the airplane in good condition and teach Houdini how to fly.

Twice nightly at the Hansa Theater, Houdini performed the Water Can Escape. Each morning he kept busy learning how to fly. German Army officials let him use the Hufaren military parade grounds at Wandsbek as an airfield. Finally, one calm, cloudless November morning, Houdini was ready to make his first flight. He climbed into the Voisin's pilot's seat and grasped the steering wheel. Brassac spun the wooden propeller. The engine roared, and soon the plane shot forward. It rose several feet into the air before a gust of wind roughly pushed it back to earth. Houdini recorded in his diary, "I smashed the machine. Broke Propeller all to hell."[9]

Brassac ordered a new propeller from Paris. Within two weeks, Houdini was ready to try again. On November 26, 1909, he made his first successful flight over the Hufaren parade grounds. After that, he made short flights every day. Thrilled with flying, Houdini soared his airplane gracefully through the air.

On to Australia

Houdini's stage tour of Germany ended in December 1909. He was scheduled next to go to Melbourne, Australia. While preparing for the trip, Houdini learned that no one had ever flown an airplane in Australia. He decided he was going to be the first. Brassac packed the Voisin in shipping crates for the long ocean journey.

The steamship *Malwa* sailed from Marseilles, France, on January 7, 1910. The ship crossed the Mediterranean Sea and passed through the Suez Canal. As always, Houdini was seasick most of the time. But while crossing the Indian Ocean he felt well enough one evening to give a magic show for the passengers. "I am as good as when I was young!" he happily declared in a letter.[10] Altogether, though, the twenty-nine-day voyage was a miserable experience. Unable to eat during most of the trip, Houdini lost twenty-eight pounds.

On February 6, the *Malwa* reached Adelaide, Australia. Houdini, Bess, and Brassac traveled by train four hundred miles to Melbourne. Houdini quickly used his proven method to get newspaper

Witnesses cheer as Houdini flies his Voisin biplane at the Hufaren military parade grounds on November 26, 1909. Houdini soon decided that he would be the first to fly an airplane in Australia.

publicity for his Melbourne theater engagement. He leaped in handcuffs and leg irons from the city's Queens Bridge into the Yarra River before a crowd of twenty thousand. On February 7, he began two months of performances at the New Opera House. Posters out front called Houdini's show, "Absolutely the Greatest and most Sensational Act that has ever been engaged by any Manager."[11]

Digger's Rest

For the moment, however, Houdini's greatest interest remained flying. Brassac unpacked the Voisin and assembled the airplane at Digger's Rest, a field twenty miles from Melbourne. "I stand a chance," Houdini excitedly wrote home, "of being the First Flier in this country."[12]

Houdini hurried to Digger's Rest after his last show each evening. Each morning he woke up hoping to get into the air. He had to wait two weeks for perfect weather. At daybreak on March 16, 1910, the Voisin was positioned on the planks that served as the plane's runway. Behind the steering wheel, Houdini fitted a pair of goggles over his eyes. He signaled that he was ready, and Brassac spun the propeller. The engine roared to life. When Brassac released the mooring rope, the plane shot forward and up, into the wind. The plane nearly hit the top of a tall gum tree at the edge of the field. Houdini pushed forward on the elevating control just in time. Flying at fifty miles an hour, the plane circled the field at a height of twenty-five feet for five minutes. Then Houdini steered back to the plank runway for a smooth landing. Witnesses broke out cheering. Harry Houdini had made the first successful airplane flight in Australia. Before the day ended, he made two more brief flights. That night, he excitedly recorded in his diary: "Never in any fear and never in any danger. It is a wonderful thing."[13]

Houdini was thrilled with his success. He wrote a magician friend, "Even if history forgets Houdini, the Handcuff King, it must write my name as the first man to fly here."[14] On March 21, he stayed in the air a full seven minutes and thirty-seven seconds. But he soon lost his interest in flying. He had been the first to fly in Australia and that was enough for him. He turned his attention to other challenges.

6

DEATH-
DEFYING
ENTERTAINER

"I want to be first . . .," Houdini told a newspaper reporter in 1910. "First in my profession. . . . For that I give all the thought, all the power that is in me. . . . I have struggled and fought. . . . I have tortured my body and risked my life only for that. . . ."[1] At the end of his Australian tour, he and Bess sailed across the Pacific Ocean to the United States. They finally arrived in New York City in July 1910, in time to celebrate his mother's sixty-ninth birthday.

Houdini's visit lasted less than a month. He had promised to return to Europe. When he and Bess arrived in Great Britain, he discovered other magicians were now performing the Water Can Escape.

Once again, he needed a new trick to keep audiences excited about him.

The Water Torture Cell

"I believe it is the climax of all my studies and labors," Houdini wrote. "Never will I be able to construct anything that will be more dangerous or difficult for me to do."[2] After careful thought, Houdini described to his assistant, James Collins, what he needed, and Collins built it for him. Houdini called the new stunt the Water Torture Cell. But he privately called it "the Upside-Down" or "U.S.D."[3]

Houdini first performed his amazing new trick in 1912, at the Circus Busch in Berlin. The Water Torture Cell was a glass-fronted tank. He invited audience members onto the stage to inspect the tank. The tank was then filled with water while Houdini changed into a bathing suit offstage. When he returned, he lay flat on the floor. His assistants locked his ankles in wooden stocks with metal bindings. With ropes and pulleys, he was hauled into the air. Soon, he hung upside down above the tank. Then he was lowered, headfirst, into the water, and the stocks were secured to the tank. The magician's curtained cabinet was placed around the tank and the audience waited.

reporters crowded the East River pier where Houdini promised to perform his stunt. Cecilia Weiss was also there to watch her famous son defy death.

At the last moment, however, some policemen arrived. They announced that jumping off piers in New York was against the law. Houdini immediately boarded a tugboat. He would perform his stunt in the harbor. Once out in the open water, the reporters aboard the tugboat examined the handcuffs and leg irons and locked them on Houdini. Houdini was assisted into the box and the top was nailed on. James Collins gave commands as the box was lowered into the water. It took Houdini fifty-seven seconds to escape and bob up to the surface. The reporters burst into cheers. The box was raised from the water. When it was opened, the handcuffs and leg irons were still inside. The stunt got headlines in all of the local newspapers. That evening, New Yorkers flocked to Hammerstein's Roof Garden to see Houdini do the box escape in the large pool located beneath the stage there.

Houdini's Good-bye to His Mother

After his success at Hammerstein's Roof Garden, Houdini returned to Europe. In the summer of 1913, he briefly came back to New York to play another two weeks at Hammerstein's Roof Garden.

He made the trip home mostly because it gave him a chance to visit with his mother. Cecilia Weiss sat in the front row and beamed while he escaped from straitjackets and the Water Torture Cell.

On July 8, 1913, Houdini and Bess boarded a ship bound for Europe so he could resume his tour. Bess Houdini described the emotional scene when Houdini parted with his mother:

> Persons at the pier beheld a curious sight. They saw Houdini clinging to a little old woman in black silk, embracing and kissing her, saying good-by and going up the gangplank, only to return to embrace her again. [His mother said to him in German,] 'Ehrich, vielleicht wenn du zurück kommst bin ich nicht hier' (Perhaps when you come home I shall not be here).[6]

The Houdinis sailed and arrived in Denmark nine days later. At the Circus Beketow, in Copenhagen, Houdini was handed a telegram. The words he read gave him such a shock that he fell to the floor unconscious. When he was revived, he sobbed, "Mama—my dear little mother—poor little mama."[7] He had learned that on July 14, 1913, his mother had suffered a stroke in Asbury Park, New Jersey. She had died on July 16, at the age of seventy-two.

Jewish tradition required that she be buried within one day of her death. But Houdini insisted that the funeral be delayed. He sent a message to his brother Theo to wait until he could get back to New

York. Houdini and Bess landed in New York City on July 29. The next day, the funeral took place at Machpelah Cemetery in Brooklyn. Houdini sadly watched as the coffin was lowered into the ground beside the grave of his father. For a month afterward, he grieved deeply for his mother. He visited the cemetery every day, throwing himself weeping on her grave. He declared, "I who have laughed at the terrors of death, who have smilingly leaped from high bridges, received a shock from which I do not think recovery is possible."[8]

At the end of August 1913, Houdini finally resumed his European tour. Throughout the autumn, he performed in Germany and France. Audiences were thrilled and amazed to watch him escape from the Water Torture Cell. When the tour ended, Houdini returned to New York. But he felt uncomfortable living on West 113th Street. Everything there reminded him of his mother. So he and Bess moved in with Theo's family in Brooklyn. The Houdinis stayed there for three and a half years, until, in February 1918, they moved back to 113th Street.

Walking Through a Brick Wall

Houdini returned for a third engagement at Hammerstein's Roof Garden in New York City in July 1914. There he introduced a new trick. He called it simply Walking Through a Brick Wall. While the audience watched, a crew of bricklayers constructed a real wall of bricks and mortar onstage. When finished, it stood ten feet long and nine feet high. They built this wall on a steel beam mounted on small wheels. The beam raised the wall three inches from the carpeted floor. A committee from the audience was invited onstage to see that the wall was truly solid.

Committee members were told to stand at each corner of the carpet. A drumroll played as Houdini stepped to one side of the wall. His assistants brought forward screens, which blocked the wall from view. Houdini waved his hands above the left-hand screen and called out, "Now I'm going." His hands disappeared, and several seconds later they popped up above the right-hand screen on the opposite side of the wall. "Here I am," he cried. He drew away the screen to show that he had done the impossible. He had walked through a brick wall. The audience sat in silent astonishment.[9]

The secret of the trick was very simple. The brick wall was built over a trapdoor in the stage, which was covered by the carpet. While Houdini took position behind the screen, James Collins, below stage, opened the trapdoor. Even though committee members stood at the carpet corners, the carpet was still loose enough to sag. The space was just deep enough for Houdini to crawl under the wall to the other side. Then Collins shut the trapdoor again.[10]

The Suspended Straitjacket Escape

"The easiest way to attract a crowd," Houdini once declared, "is to let it be known that at a given time and a given place someone is going to attempt something that in the event of failure will mean sudden death."[11] Starting in the autumn of 1915, Houdini did a series of straitjacket escapes while dangling by his ankles from the tops of skyscrapers. In whatever city he happened to be playing, he arranged to do the stunt from the leading newspaper's building. He always got his picture on the newspaper's front page, and people flocked to see his stage show.

Even though he always made careful preparations, it was a dangerous stunt. The *Boston Post* described,

> A number of times his body, held taut by the strait-jacket, was swung towards the building by the wind, while a murmur of fear arose from the crowd. A minute, two minutes passed, and the crowd roared. Houdini's body, held rigid by the strait-jacket, was beginning to move. Slowly, but surely, the man who has startled the entire world by his feats and by his magic, began to work himself free.[12]

Hanging upside down, high above the street, Houdini would twist and arch his body. At last, the

People in the street below stare in wonder as Houdini dangles in a straitjacket from a building in Washington, D.C. His suspended straitjacket escapes were dangerous but got him lots of free publicity.

straitjacket would come free and drop to the street far below.

Fifty thousand people crammed the streets of downtown Baltimore to see him do the stunt on April 26, 1916. When Houdini finally freed himself, the crowd went wild. Still dangling on the rope, Houdini smiled, stretched out his arms, and took a bow upside down. In Washington, D.C., one hundred thousand people watched him wriggle free while hanging from the Munsey Building. The *Washington Times* explained that this was "the biggest crowd ever assembled in Washington at one place except for the inauguration of a President."[13]

World War I

World War I had raged in Europe since 1914. In April 1917, after German submarines had sunk a number of American ships, the United States entered the war. America joined forces with Great

Tight Places

From time to time, President Woodrow Wilson found himself in tricky political situations. Wilson saw Houdini perform his magic act at Keith's Theatre in Washington, D.C., in 1915. After the show, he met Houdini. "I envy your ability to escape from tight places," Wilson jokingly told him. "Sometimes I wish I were able to do the same."[14]

Britain, France, Russia, and other Allied nations. Together, they would fight the enemy Central Powers, which included Germany, Austria-Hungary, Bulgaria, and the Ottoman Empire. On June 11, Houdini excitedly wrote to a friend, "I register tomorrow for enlisting. HURRAH, now I am one of the boys."[15] Houdini was still in excellent health. But at the age of forty-three, he soon discovered that military officials considered him too old to serve.

Still, Houdini found ways to help the war effort. He visited training camps and military hospitals and entertained the troops. He called his favorite trick Money for Nothing.[16] He made five-dollar gold pieces magically appear at the tips of his fingers. He often gave the coins away to soldiers just about to leave for Europe. He gave away more than seven thousand dollars of his own money to grateful soldiers in this way. In addition, he sold one million dollars worth of Liberty Bonds at public rallies. When people bought Liberty Bonds, they were loaning the government money with which to fight the war. Houdini joined in the celebrations when World War I ended with Allied victory in November 1918.

The Vanishing Elephant

It was in the huge entertainment hall the Hippodrome, in New York City, that Houdini first made an elephant disappear on January 7, 1918. The advertisement declared, "The Most Colossal Disappearing Mystery that History Records. Dissolving into thin air, on the largest stage in the world, an elephant weighing 10,000 pounds. Before one's very eyes . . ." [17] Making doves and rabbits disappear were old magician's tricks. But no one had ever made an elephant disappear.

During the performance, the elephant's trainer led the great beast into a huge box, which was then closed. Houdini waved his arms and shouted mystical words, and when the box was opened, the elephant was gone. "Matinee crowds will worry themselves into sleep nightly wondering what Houdini did with his elephant," exclaimed *Variety* magazine. [18] Curious people often pestered Houdini to reveal how he did this seemingly impossible trick. He always replied, "Even the elephant doesn't know how it is done." [19] The Vanishing Elephant trick was an overwhelming success, and Houdini performed it at the Hippodrome for nearly five months.

7

MOVIE STAR

" I have signed to play the star part of a big serial movie," Houdini wrote to a friend.[1] In June 1918, Houdini became a movie actor. He signed a contract with producer B. A. Rolfe of Octagon Films to star in a fifteen-part silent serial, or a film with a series of episodes, called *The Master Mystery*. Houdini helped to write the scripts.

The Master Mystery

The entire series was filmed in Yonkers, New York, in just six weeks. Houdini played the role of Quentin Locke, an undercover agent for the Department of Justice. Locke's enemy is an evil millionaire businessman who is determined to promote his interests regardless of the law. In each thrilling episode, Houdini's character faced danger and death.

Quentin Locke escaped from straitjackets, handcuffs, and ropes. In one episode, he was tied at the bottom of an elevator shaft. He had to free himself before the elevator car dropped down to crush him. In another episode, he survived being nailed into a packing crate and tossed into the sea. Locke made a third escape after being strapped into an electric chair. Whether buried alive in a gravel pit or dangled upside down over a vat of boiling acid, Locke always managed to escape.

The plots were silly, and Houdini's acting skills were not very good. But Locke's thrilling escapes kept audiences at the edge of their seats. Each episode of *The Master Mystery* gave people a glimpse of how Houdini did his tricks, such as untying knots with his toes.

The Grim Game

The public flocked to see *The Master Mystery*, and it was a great success. Jesse Lasky, a producer at Paramount Pictures, soon signed Houdini to act in two full-length movies. Houdini traveled to Hollywood, California, to film the first movie, *The Grim Game*, in the spring of 1919.

In this poster advertising The Master Mystery, *a chained Houdini is being threatened by a robot. Movie audiences enjoyed watching Houdini escape from impossible dangers.*

The Grim Game's murder-mystery plot called for Houdini's character to defy death repeatedly. One advertisement gave audiences an idea of the kind of excitement they could expect:

> SEE him dive between the wheels of a speeding motor-truck and foil his pursuers!
> SEE him climb the side of a prison and crawl for a rope to the end of a flagpole swaying far from earth!
> SEE him on the brink of a gorge, fight a terrifying battle with his foes!
> SEE him leap from the roof of a skyscraper and release himself from a straight-jacket while hanging head downward on a rope!
> SEE him risk his life in a deadly bear-trap and set himself free![2]

Terror Island

Houdini's second movie for Jesse Lasky was also filmed in California, in Hollywood and on Catalina Island, in the autumn of 1919. The plot of *Terror Island* called for Houdini to play the role of wealthy inventor Harry Harper. During the course of the movie, Harper finds a case of stolen diamonds in a sunken ship. He also saves the heroine's father from a tribe of terrifying cannibals.

As a movie star, Houdini became more famous than ever. The London Palladium offered him a weekly salary of $3,750 to come to England to perform. The contract would make Houdini the highest-paid entertainer in the world. He accepted the offer, and in December 1919, he sailed for England.

Sir Arthur Conan Doyle

While performing in England, Houdini met and became friends with Sir Arthur Conan Doyle. Doyle was the author of the hugely successful Sherlock Holmes mystery stories. At the time, Houdini and Doyle were two of the most famous people in the world. Doyle said of his new friend, "Houdini is far and away the most curious and intriguing character whom I have ever encountered."[3]

Both men shared a keen interest in spiritualism. Spiritualists believed it was possible to make contact with the dead. People called spirit mediums claimed that they were able to make the contacts. At spirit meetings called séances, mediums appeared to make strange voices speak through megaphones, and to cause other spirit activity to occur in darkened rooms. Spiritualism had become extremely popular after World War I, because so many people mourned loved ones who had died during the war. Sir Arthur Conan Doyle had turned to spiritualism because his son, Kingsley, had died in the fighting. Houdini recalled, "Sir Arthur told me he had spoken six times to his son."[4]

Houdini was fascinated by spiritualism. But he felt certain that most mediums were fakes. He and Bess had themselves posed as mediums years earlier while performing with Thomas Hill's traveling medicine show. Still, Houdini wanted to believe spirit contact was possible. "There is no sacrifice I would not make to be able to get in communication with my mother," he declared.[5] Since his mother's death, Houdini had attended many séances. But failure to make true contact with her spirit made him bitter and skeptical.

Doyle recommended a number of spirit mediums, and Houdini attended one hundred séances in England. The

Sir Arthur Conan Doyle, pictured here, became famous writing mystery stories featuring detective Sherlock Holmes. In 1919, Houdini and Doyle became friends because they both had an interest in spiritualism.

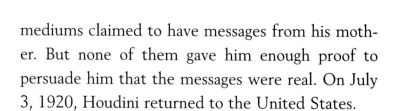

The Fox Sisters

The spiritualist movement began in Hydesville, New York, in 1848. For several nights strange rapping sounds were heard in the farmhouse where John Fox lived with his wife and their two daughters, Katie and Margaret, aged twelve and fifteen. On the night of March 31, one of the girls snapped her fingers and the supposed spirit answered with an equal number of raps. In the following days, the girls got the spirit to answer questions they asked (one rap meaning yes, two raps meaning no). Visitors to the house described how invisible hands slapped at them in the dark. They felt the floor vibrate and saw window shades roll up, drawers fly open, and other spirit evidence. Thousands of people came to believe the Fox sisters had a special talent to communicate with the spirit world. Only years later did Margaret Fox admit that she and her sister had done everything with tricks. The spirit rappings, for example, had been done by cracking the joints of their big toes.

mediums claimed to have messages from his mother. But none of them gave him enough proof to persuade him that the messages were real. On July 3, 1920, Houdini returned to the United States.

The Man From Beyond

At the start of 1921, Houdini formed the Houdini Picture Corporation to make movies on his own. He hired his brother Theo to run the company. Their first production was called *The Man From Beyond*. Houdini wrote the story and acted the starring role. His character, Howard Hillary, is found frozen inside a block of Arctic ice. He has been frozen for one hundred years, since being shipwrecked in 1820. Hillary's body is thawed, and he returns to life. The film describes his efforts to understand the modern world.

The most exciting scene in the movie showed a river rescue at Niagara Falls. The heroine, while canoeing, seems headed for the great falls. Hillary bravely swims to save her from certain death. *Variety* magazine exclaimed the scene had "a whale of a punch."[6] The *New York World* reviewer declared he "quivered at the views of the couple battling in the rapids . . . and almost cheered when they made the crawl to safety."[7]

The Man From Beyond opened in New York City in April 1922. To attract huge audiences to the theater, Houdini appeared each night in person and presented a complete stage show. He performed the Vanishing Elephant, the Needle Trick, and the Straitjacket Escape. He also performed two new illusions called Goodbye Winter and Welcome Summer.

In Goodbye Winter, Bess Houdini, dressed in winter furs, balanced on top of three stacked tables.

In this picture taken from The Man From Beyond, *Houdini's character is discovered frozen. To help sell tickets in New York City, Houdini treated audiences to a live stage show each night.*

Houdini mounted a ladder and covered her with a cloth. When he pulled the cloth away, he shouted, "Goodbye Winter!" and Bess had disappeared.

In Welcome Summer, a large wooden cone with an opening in it was shown to be empty. Houdini shot a pistol and shouted, "Welcome Summer!" Suddenly a girl appeared inside the cone, covered with flowers.

Houdini made personal appearances in Washington, Detroit, and Buffalo to help attract crowds to *The Man From Beyond*. Even these live shows, however, failed to make the movie a hit. Too many people thought the story and the acting were silly.

A Fateful Séance

In April 1922, Sir Arthur Conan Doyle, with his wife and three children, arrived in New York. Doyle had come to the United States to give a lecture tour on spiritualism. Houdini and Bess joined the Doyles for a short seaside vacation. They stayed at the Ambassador Hotel in Atlantic City, New Jersey. Houdini never forgot the afternoon of June 17. "As Sir Arthur, Mrs. Houdini and I were sitting on the sand . . . with the children," he reported,

> Sir Arthur excused himself saying that he was going to have his usual afternoon nap. He left us but returned in a short time and said "Houdini, if agreeable, Lady Doyle will give you a special séance, as she has a feeling that she might have a message coming through. At any rate, she is willing to try."[8]

Doyle believed his wife had natural skill as a spirit medium. Houdini was willing to learn if it were true. The two men went to the Doyles' hotel room. Doyle pulled down the window shades to darken the room. It was thought that spirits communicated better in darkness. Houdini recalled, "We three, Lady Doyle, Sir Arthur and I, sat around the table on which were a number of pencils and a writing pad, placing our hands on the surface of the table."[9]

During the séance, Lady Doyle believed that she had contacted Houdini's mother. She scribbled words that she claimed the spirit communicated directly through her hand: "Oh, my darling, thank God, thank God, at last I'm through—I've tried, oh so often—now I am happy. Why, of course, I want to talk to my boy—my own beloved boy."[10]

Houdini read the sheets of paper as quickly as Lady Doyle wrote them. "I was willing to believe, even wanted to believe," he later explained. ". . . I especially wanted to speak to my Mother, because that day, June 17 . . . was her birthday."[11] The message from his mother, however, did not mention her birthday. It did not give any detailed information about her at all. It was written in English, a language his mother could not write. Houdini also noticed a Christian cross drawn at the top of the first page. But his mother, of course, was Jewish.

At the end of the séance, he silently left the darkened hotel room, deeply disappointed. He did not believe he had made contact with his mother. He hid his feelings from the Doyles when he said good-bye to them on June 24, and they sailed home to England.

Exposing Fake Mediums

Houdini came to a decision after his failure to reach his mother's spirit. He spent more and more time describing spiritualism to his theater audiences and revealing onstage the tricks of fake mediums. He claimed no one knew more about their trickery than he did. He offered a five-thousand-dollar prize to any medium who could do anything he could not do with tricks.

In November 1922, Houdini published an article in the *New York Sun* attacking spiritualism. In it, he told of his disappointing séance with the Doyles. "I feel rather sore about it," Doyle wrote angrily.[12] As Houdini continued to attack fake mediums, his friendship with Doyle ended. In another public statement, Houdini declared, "I can truthfully say that I have never seen a mystery, and I have never visited a séance, which I could not fully explain."[13] Houdini threw himself into this new work of exposing fake mediums with the energy and purpose of a man on a crusade.

8

CRUSADER AGAINST SPIRITUALIST FRAUDS

At the end of 1922, *Haldane of the Secret Service* opened in theaters. It was the second movie to be produced by Houdini's film company. This time, Houdini starred as Secret Service agent Heath Haldane. In the movie, Haldane battles a gang of international counterfeiters and drug smugglers. The gang captures Haldane and ties him to the side of a huge turning waterwheel. Haldane frees himself just as he is about to be crushed. Houdini actively promoted the film. But because the waterwheel escape was the only exciting thing in the movie, *Haldane of the Secret Service* did not sell a lot of tickets.

The *Scientific American*

In December 1922, Orson Munn, the publisher of the *Scientific American* magazine, offered a prize. He would give $2,500 to the first person producing scientific proof of spirits. Houdini was invited to join the committee that would judge the competition.

The first person to try for the prize was George Valiantine. He gave two séances for the committee while Houdini was away on tour. During these séances, a megaphone floated about the completely darkened room and tapped committee members on their heads. Houdini hurried to New York in time to attend the third séance. This time, unknown to

Houdini demonstrates how a fake medium can ring a bell. Even though his hands and feet are "controlled," Houdini has slipped his right foot out of his shoe and picked up the bell with his toes.

Valiantine, his chair had been wired. If he left his seat during the séance, a light would secretly flash. It soon became clear that whenever spirit activity occurred in the darkened room Valiantine was not in his chair. There was no doubt Valiantine was moving about in the dark, tapping people with the megaphone. As a result, Houdini publicly declared him a fake.

Another person to try for the prize was Nino Pecoraro, a twenty-four-year-old medium from Naples, Italy. During Pecoraro's first séance in a darkened room, bells mysteriously rang and tambourines jingled, even though Pecoraro was tied to his chair. Houdini insisted on attending the medium's next séance. He was surprised to discover committee members preparing to tie Pecoraro into his chair with one long piece of rope. Houdini declared that this was an easy way for someone to get free. Instead, he cut the rope into short lengths and tied the medium himself. During the séance, Pecoraro, while tightly tied into his chair, was unable to produce any spirit activity.

On a Lecture Tour

In February 1924, Houdini arranged to give a series of lectures about fake mediums. "Houdini, the magician," *Billboard* magazine exclaimed, "has become Houdini, the educator!"[1] He would give twenty-five lectures in cities across the United States.

Before each lecture, he performed outdoor stunts and challenge escapes to attract crowds. Then, during the lectures, he entertainingly revealed how fake mediums produced their effects. Using trickery, he made tables rise into the air. He made musical instruments mysteriously play and messages magically appear on blank slates. Then he showed how the tricks were done. Audiences were amazed.

In April 1924, Houdini celebrated his fiftieth birthday. A visitor remembered meeting the famous magician soon afterward. "He is not a large man and, as he himself will frankly tell you, not a particularly young one, but he is well built, and so full of energy and enthusiasm. . . . At fifty he not only looks but seems forty."[2]

In that same month, Houdini published a new book entitled *A Magician Among the Spirits*. The book attacked spiritualism and described the methods fake mediums often used. Fake mediums often paid spies to learn about their clients' private lives. Waiters in restaurants or household servants, for example, could easily overhear private conversations. One medium paid a quiet couple to sit among mourners at funerals. Another owned a beauty parlor where local gossip was overheard. Some mediums tapped telephones and opened private mail. It bothered Houdini that trusting people were being cheated. "I am pleased to see these frauds being exposed," he declared in his book, "whether I do it or someone else."[3]

Margery

To attract more interest, the *Scientific American* raised the prize it offered for proof of spirit activity to five thousand dollars. In the autumn of 1923, J. Malcolm Bird, an editor at the magazine, learned of a new medium gaining a reputation. Twenty-six-year-old Mina Crandon of Boston, Massachusetts, was the wife of a surgeon, Dr. Leroi Goddard Crandon. She was a charming, clever, and attractive woman.

Mina Crandon agreed to be investigated, but she claimed she was not interested in the prize money. To keep her life private, she asked that her identity be kept secret as long as possible. Bird agreed, and she was given the name "Margery" in magazine descriptions.

Walter the Unfriendly Spirit

The Margery séances began in April 1924 at the Crandons' home in Boston. Dr. Crandon always "controlled" Margery's right hand. That meant he held her hand to prove she did not use it to do tricks. An investigating committee member controlled her left hand. The séances took place in total darkness. Margery wore nothing but a silk robe, which she usually took off once the lights were out. She conducted her séances completely naked.

As a result of Margery's apparent talent as a spirit medium, committee members at her séances heard bugle calls and the sound of a rattling chain. Flashes of light appeared in the dark, and a clock stopped ticking when she concentrated on it. She also produced a spirit voice. She went into a trance, and her brother Walter spoke through her lips. Walter had been crushed to death by a train ten years earlier. Walter's spirit had a loud, gruff voice that was often rude. Committee member Dr. Daniel Comstock declared, "One time I placed one hand over Mrs. Crandon's mouth and

As a spirit medium, Mina Crandon, or "Margery," baffled members of the Scientific American *investigating committee, until Houdini began attending her séances and discovering her tricks.*

nose, and the other over Dr. Crandon's mouth and nose, and pressed hard, so hard that I must have hurt them. And Walter's voice—a hoarse whisper—came as clearly as it did before."[4]

Houdini Investigates

Houdini demanded that he be allowed to attend some séances with Margery. On July 23, 1924, he and other committee members sat with Margery in total darkness. Houdini sat on Margery's left, controlling her left hand. He also kept contact under the table with her left foot. Malcolm Bird controlled her right hand and foot. Other members of the committee sat with their hands touching around the table. At the center of the table lay a megaphone.

Houdini had prepared for the séance. All that day he had secretly worn an elastic bandage bound tightly around his right calf. He only took it off before leaving for the séance. The tight bandage caused his calf to become swollen and tender. His calf was so sore that he could feel the slightest touch against it. The moment the lights went out, he rolled up his trouser leg to his knee. Earlier, a bell-box had been placed on the floor between his feet. The box contained an electric bell. The bell could be rung by pressing a wooden flap on the top of the box. Walter's spirit, it was reported, could make the bell ring.

As the séance progressed, Houdini felt sure that Margery's left foot slowly began to move. He could feel her leg gently sliding against his sensitive calf. Gradually her toe reached the bell-box lid, and suddenly the bell rang. "I positively felt the tendons of her leg flex and tighten as she repeatedly touched the ringing apparatus," Houdini later declared. "There is no question in my mind about it. She did this. Then, when the ringing was over, I plainly felt her leg slide back into its original position with her foot on the floor beside mine."[5]

A little while later, Walter's spirit voice called out of the darkness, "The megaphone is in the air. Have Houdini tell me where to throw it."

"Towards me," Houdini commanded.[6]

The megaphone suddenly landed at his feet. Houdini quickly guessed how Margery had made the megaphone move. For a second, Malcolm Bird had let go of her right hand. She used that moment in the pitch-black darkness to pick up the megaphone and put it on her head like a dunce cap. When Houdini asked for the megaphone to be thrown toward him, she simply jerked her head, making it drop at his feet. "Of course with the megaphone on her head it was easy and simple," Houdini later explained. ". . . This is the slickest [trick] I have ever detected."[7]

A Second Séance

The following evening, July 24, a second séance was held in Dr. Comstock's room at the Charlesgate Hotel. Again Houdini held Margery's left hand, while Dr. Crandon grasped her right. The door was locked, and the lights were turned off. Soon there were signs of spirit activity. The bell-box, which sat on the table, mysteriously fell to the floor. Houdini felt a tap on his knee and Walter's voice exclaimed, "Ha, ha, Houdini."[8]

Then the table began to move back and forth in the dark. It rose on two legs and dropped back again. Houdini let go his left hand, which Orson Munn was holding, and felt under the table. He discovered that by leaning forward in her chair Margery had ducked her head under the table. She suddenly raised her head and tipped the table completely over. Everyone at the séance was startled, but not Houdini. He later wrote to a friend, "There is no doubt in my mind . . . that this lady . . . has been 'fooling' the scientists for months."[9]

The Control Cabinet

A month later, on August 25, the Crandons met with the investigating committee again at Dr. Comstock's hotel room. There was an important difference at the séance this time. Houdini and his assistant, James Collins, had built a wooden cabinet.

It was large enough for Margery to sit in. It was designed with holes through which she could stick both her head and her arms. Margery seated herself inside the cabinet. Houdini took her left hand while another committee member held her right. The bell-box lay on the table in front of her. Locked inside the cabinet, Margery was now challenged to produce some spirit activity.

Out of the darkness Walter's voice soon shouted at Houdini, "You think you're smart, don't you? How much are they paying you for stopping the phenomena here?"[10] Dr. Crandon accused Houdini of tampering with the bell-box in order to make his wife look bad. There was a sound of wood cracking in the darkness. When the lights were switched on, it was discovered that the cabinet was broken open. Houdini accused Margery of doing it, and the séance ended in confusion.

The next day, Collins repaired the damaged cabinet. Another séance was held that evening, August 26. Out of the darkness, Walter's voice spoke angrily again. He swore at Houdini, claiming a folding ruler had been left in the cabinet to make it look like Margery was cheating. The lights were switched on. Inside the cabinet near Margery's feet, a carpenter's ruler was found. Houdini believed that Margery had hoped to get the ruler through the neck hole. By

Houdini sits inside the control cabinet. The control cabinet was designed to prevent Margery from using trickery during her séances. On the table in front of the cabinet sits a bell-box.

holding it with her teeth, she might have been able to reach the bell-box on the table.

That night, while locked in the cabinet, Margery was unable to produce any spirit activity. Houdini later declared, "We must pay a compliment to Mrs. Crandon. . . . She certainly was clever in [pulling] the wool over the eyes of the committeemen. However, I detected her in fraud at every [séance] I attended."[11] On February 11, 1925, the investigating committee finally voted that Margery did not qualify for the *Scientific American* prize.

The Complete Entertainer

On September 14, 1925, at the Shubert Alvin Theatre in Pittsburgh, Houdini presented for the first time a magic show that used all of his talents. In the first part of the show, he performed magic tricks. The audience applauded when he made a glowing lamp disappear beneath a silk handkerchief. They gasped when he turned a beautiful girl into a flowering rosebush. With quick movements, Houdini made coins appear on his fingertips and playing cards vanish. He made rabbits suddenly appear, as well as swimming goldfish in a bowl. Then he called Bess to his side. He introduced her as his dear traveling companion of the last thirty-one years. Together, they performed Metamorphosis.

In the second part of his show he did escapes. He made spectacular escapes from crates, coffins, and other containers, and he always did the Water Torture Cell. He spent the third part of the show revealing the tricks of fake spirit mediums. As the show toured successfully from city to city, audiences agreed, Houdini could do everything well. He was a magician, an escape artist, and an exposer of frauds all rolled into one fabulous entertainer.

Rahman Bey

In March 1926, Houdini heard about a new performer in New York City named Rahman Bey. Rahman Bey called himself the Egyptian Miracle Worker. Onstage, Bey pushed needles through his cheeks and skewers into his arms and chest. Lying across a bed of nails, he let an assistant stand on his stomach. While resting on a row of swords, Bey allowed an assistant to smash a cement slab to pieces on his chest with a hammer. Houdini knew how he did these tricks. He had seen sideshow performers stick needles and skewers through their flesh without seriously injuring themselves. He knew a person could safely lie on a bed of nails, if the nails were set close together. He also guessed the sword blades Rahman Bey rested on were too dull to hurt him.

But Rahman Bey performed one trick that baffled Houdini. Bey fell into a trance and stiffly dropped back into the arms of two assistants. They lowered his body into a zinc coffin and sealed the lid. The assistants then shoveled sand over the coffin until it was completely covered. Rahman Bey claimed he could slow his breathing until it was almost stopped. He could survive inside the nearly airless coffin because he went into a state of suspended animation. It was said that the coffin contained enough air to last only three minutes. Bey's assistants waited ten minutes before removing the sand. As if rising from the dead, the Egyptian sat up in the coffin. Later, at a private swimming pool on Fifty-ninth Street, Bey stayed underwater in the coffin a full hour. Newspapers headlined the story, and Houdini was publicly challenged to equal the stunt.

Houdini boldly announced he would give it a try. He had an iron coffin built the same size as Rahman Bey's. It was six feet six inches long, twenty-two inches wide, and twenty-two inches high. He equipped it with a telephone and an emergency electric bell. For three weeks, Houdini tested the coffin in the basement of his house. Finally, on August 5, 1926, he invited newspaper reporters to the swimming pool of the Shelton Hotel at 49th Street and Lexington Avenue.

Houdini allowed himself to be sealed inside the airtight coffin, and it was lowered into the water. An official timekeeper kept track of the passing minutes. Fifteen minutes went by, half an hour, then forty-five minutes. Houdini remained in the coffin. Even after he equaled Rahman Bey's record of one hour, he remained underwater. After an hour and fifteen minutes, suddenly the telephone rang. James Collins answered it, and Houdini explained that although the coffin was slowly leaking, he would stay inside even longer. It was one and a half hours before the coffin was finally raised from the pool and opened. Houdini sat up, soaking wet, exhausted, but alive.

Houdini told the reporters that there was nothing remarkable in what he had done. "Any one can do it," he insisted. "The important thing is to believe that you are safe, don't breathe too deeply, and don't make any unnecessary movements."[12] If a person did these things, the air in the coffin would last.

After the experiment, Houdini ordered an expensive bronze coffin built. He announced that he would perform the stunt using the bronze coffin during his autumn tour. Privately he told his friends, however, that he felt death was looming over him. If his strange sensation proved correct, he wished to be buried in the coffin. In September 1926, Houdini set out on what would be his last national tour.

9

THE FINAL PERFORMANCE

At the age of fifty-two, Houdini remained in perfect health. Constant exercise kept him strong, and he had never drunk alcohol or smoked tobacco. Unfortunately, on October 11, 1926, in Albany, New York, while performing the Water Torture Cell, an accident occurred. His assistants, James Collins and James Vickery, fastened him in the stocks and began to raise him into the air. Suddenly he felt a jolt of pain in his left ankle. A doctor from the audience found that Houdini's ankle had been broken.

Despite the injury, Houdini insisted on finishing the show. Late that night he finally went to the hospital and allowed the ankle to be set and put in a cast. His tour continued, and he opened at the Princess Theatre in Montreal, Canada, on October 18. While his ankle mended, he could not perform the Water Torture Cell, but audiences warmly applauded the rest of his show.

Fateful Punches

On the day of October 19, Houdini lectured to students at McGill University, in Montreal. He had been invited by the psychology department. He

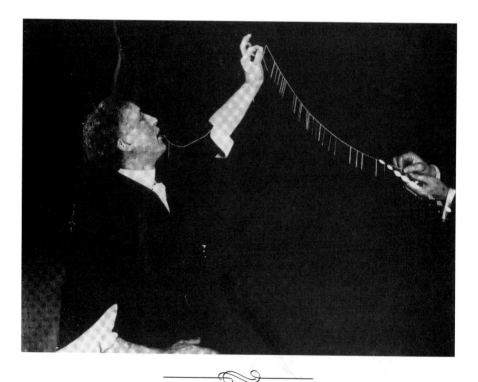

In his fifties, Houdini was still performing The Needle Trick. He learned the trick at the Columbian Exposition in Chicago in 1893 and performed it successfully throughout his long career.

talked about his experiences exposing fake mediums. After the lecture, he chatted with faculty members and students. One student, Samuel J. Smiley, stepped forward with a pencil sketch of Houdini. He had made it during the lecture. Houdini liked the drawing. He invited Smiley to visit him at the Princess Theatre to draw a more detailed portrait.

Smiley, along with a fellow student named Jack Price, arrived at the theater on Friday morning, October 22. Houdini invited them backstage into his dressing room. While Houdini relaxed on a couch reading his mail, Smiley began to sketch him. Before long, another McGill University student, J. Gordon Whitehead, tapped on the door. He was bringing back a book that Houdini had loaned him.

"Is it true," Whitehead asked Houdini, "that you are so strong you can take a punch anywhere on your body without injury?"[1]

Houdini had always been proud of his strength. He said that it was true. Whitehead asked if he could test this claim by punching him. Taking care of his broken ankle, Houdini slowly began to rise from the couch. Before he had time to prepare himself, however, Whitehead began throwing punches at his stomach with all his might.

"This student," Jack Price later recalled, ". . . gave Houdini some very hammer-like blows below the belt. . . . at least four very hard and severe body blows."

Price yelled, "Hey there. You must be crazy, what are you doing?"[2]

Houdini gestured that he had had enough. The look on his face revealed that the punches had hurt. Smiley and Price pulled Whitehead away. Houdini insisted that he was all right, and the three students left together. During the next hours, though, Houdini noticed his stomach had begun to ache. When he performed his show that evening, he was in real pain. He felt so bad that night that he got little sleep. He complained to Bess that he thought he had a strained muscle or had developed a cramp.

The Show Must Go On

Houdini was scheduled to bring his show to Detroit the following evening, October 23. Traveling west on the train, he felt so bad that Bess telegraphed ahead. She arranged for a doctor to meet them at their Detroit hotel. The doctor would examine Houdini when they arrived. Unfortunately, the train reached Detroit late, and the Houdinis hurried directly to the Garrick Theater.

Dr. Leo Kretzka waited at the Statler Hotel until he realized what had happened. Then he rushed to the theater to examine Houdini there. Houdini's dressing room contained no cot or couch. Houdini took off his clothes and lay on the floor. Dr. Kretzka knelt beside him and felt his sore abdomen. The doctor guessed Houdini was suffering from acute appendicitis. It is extremely rare to get appendicitis from a punch to the abdomen, but that seemed to be what had happened. Dr. Kretzka recommended that Houdini go to the hospital right away. Bess was out of the room at the time, and Houdini kept the doctor's opinion a secret. The theater manager had told him people were lined up outside on the sidewalk, hoping for tickets to the evening's performance. "They're here to see me," Houdini declared. "I won't disappoint them."[3] He began preparing for the show.

An Emergency Operation

During the first act of his show that night, Houdini performed magic tricks with silk handkerchiefs and coins. He also did a few card tricks. As soon as the stage curtains closed, however, he slid to his knees in pain. His assistants helped him backstage. Houdini's clothes were soaked with sweat. His temperature had risen to 104 degrees Fahrenheit. Ice packs cooled him a little, and he forced himself to return to the stage for the second act.

He performed as long as he could, but finally, he whispered painfully to his assistant, James Collins, "Drop the curtain, Collins, I can't go any further."[4]

Houdini managed to get to his dressing room and change into his street clothes. Even then, he refused to go to the hospital. Instead, he went to his hotel. Bess finally had to throw a temper tantrum in order to get her husband to agree to see a doctor. Dr. Charles S. Kennedy, chief surgeon at Grace Hospital, was called to the hotel. Kennedy urged Houdini to go to the hospital immediately. Houdini stubbornly insisted on calling his own doctor in New York first. Over the telephone, Dr. William Stone finally persuaded Houdini to get emergency hospital treatment.

On the afternoon of October 25, at Grace Hospital, Dr. Kennedy removed Houdini's ruptured appendix. It was discovered that the rupture, or tear in the appendix, had produced an infection called peritonitis. The poisonous infection was spreading through Houdini's stomach lining and surrounding organs, causing him extreme pain and weakness. The doctor grimly told newspaper reporters that he believed Houdini lay on the brink of death.

"Rosabelle, Believe"

Houdini's brothers and sister, Theo, Nat, and Gladys, rushed to Detroit. Dr. Kennedy sadly told Theo, "He will never get well."[5] The doctor performed a second operation on Houdini to drain the infected areas on October 29. Afterward, Bess was allowed into Houdini's hospital room for a visit. She approached his bedside, and he clasped her hand to his heart. He whispered, "Mother never reached me. If . . . anything happens . . . you must be prepared. Remember the message: 'Rosabelle, believe.' When you hear those words . . . know it is Houdini speaking."[6] He promised Bess that if he died, his spirit would try to contact her. "Rosabelle, believe" would be their secret signal.

Houdini battled for life for several days. Late in the morning of October 31, Theo sat beside his sick brother's bed. Houdini grasped his hand and said, "I'm tired of fighting. Guess this thing is . . . going to get me."[7] At 1:26 that afternoon, Harry Houdini died, at the age of fifty-two. Many people thought it curious that such a mystical man as Houdini should die on October 31—Halloween. According to superstition, Halloween night is the night when spirits roam the earth.

All of Houdini's baggage and props for his show had been shipped to New York. But one crate had been left behind by mistake, the crate containing the bronze coffin. Now Houdini's body was placed in the coffin and carried east by train. On November 4, 1926, two thousand people jammed into the Elks Lodge ballroom on West Forty-third Street in New York City to attend Houdini's funeral. Afterward, a hearse took the coffin to Machpelah Cemetery in

Queens. Pallbearers solemnly lowered Houdini's coffin into the ground beside the grave of his mother. As requested in his will, inside the coffin Houdini's head rested on a black bag. The bag contained loving letters that his mother had written to him during her life.

Houdini's Spirit

"If it is possible for anyone to get through after death, that person will be me," Houdini had always

Houdini's brother, Theo, and his wife, Bess, visit Houdini's grave at Machpelah Cemetery in Brooklyn, New York. Over the years, the bust of Houdini has been stolen from the grave several times.

insited.[8] For years, Bess Houdini hoped that she would be able to contact his spirit. Every Sunday at the hour of his death, she shut herself in her bedroom. She stared at a photograph of Houdini and waited for a sign. She also promised ten thousand dollars to any medium who could produce the secret message Houdini had promised to send her. No medium was ever successful. In 1935, she told a reporter,

> I receive many messages that are supposed to come from Houdini through mediums and strange séances but they never mean anything to me. Very often I go to séances, hoping and praying that the signals Houdini gave me will be heard. No message comes to me while I am waiting to hear.[9]

Each year, Bess held a special séance on October 31. She held the last one in 1936 on the roof of the Knickerbocker Hotel in Los Angeles. It was the tenth anniversary of Houdini's death. Magician Edward Saint began the ceremony. He solemnly declared, "The world is waiting, Harry. . . . All are waiting. Please speak, Harry. . . . Call to him Madame Houdini, call to him . . ." Bess then said, "Houdini, we've waited so long. Houdini, please." Her pleas were answered only by silence. At last, Bess declared, "Houdini has not come. I do not believe he will ever come."[10] After that séance, she never publicly attempted to contact him again. Bess Houdini lived until February 11, 1943. She died of a heart attack at the age of sixty-seven, while traveling by train from California to New York.

The Great Magician

People will always wonder how Houdini did so many of his thrilling escapes. After his death, Sir Arthur Conan Doyle admitted, "He was [the] great master of his profession."[11] Famed critic Edmund Wilson commented, "He certainly knew more about trickery than anyone else in the world."[12] Friend and well-known performer Will Rogers truthfully called Houdini "the greatest showman of our time by far."[13]

It was Houdini's dramatic style onstage, his skill at staying in the news, and his determination to invent new escapes year after year that kept him on people's minds. "All the world is a theater to me," Houdini had once declared.[14] During his lifetime, Houdini amazed all the world. The legend of his magical career still amazes people. Even today, whenever someone gets into a tight spot, it is often said that he or she will have to pull a "Houdini" in order to escape. It seems, after all, that Harry Houdini's spirit will remain with us forever.

CHRONOLOGY

1874—Born in Budapest, Hungary, on March 24, the son of Rabbi Mayer Samuel Weiss and Cecilia Steiner Weiss.

1876—Rabbi Weiss travels to the United States.

1878—Cecilia Weiss and the Weiss children join Rabbi Weiss in Appleton, Wisconsin.

1882—Rabbi Weiss loses his job as rabbi in Appleton, and the family moves to Milwaukee, Wisconsin.

1886—Runs away from home intending to earn money to give to his mother; Rabbi Weiss goes to New York City in search of work.

1888—Weiss family is reunited in New York City; Goes to work in a necktie factory.

1891—Reads memoirs of magician Jean-Eugene Robert-Houdin; Decides to become a professional magician; Takes stage name of Harry Houdini and performs a trick called Metamorphosis with partner Jacob Hyman and later with his brother Theo.

1893—The Houdini Brothers perform at the Columbian Exposition in Chicago, Illinois.

1894—Houdini meets and marries Wilhelmina Beatrice Rahmer, a singer and dancer whose stage name is Bessie Raymond; Bessie takes Theo's place in the magic act.

1895 –1897—The Houdinis perform with the Welsh Brothers' Circus, the American Gaiety Girls, and the California Concert Company.

1898—Houdini does his first handcuff challenge and jail escape in Chicago.

1899—The Houdinis make a successful tour of the Orpheum theatre circuit.

1900 –1904—The Houdinis travel to Europe; Houdini becomes a sensation in England, Germany, and elsewhere in Europe.

1905—Returns to the United States for successful magic tour.

1906—Escapes from assassin's cell in Washington, D.C.; Makes first handcuffed bridge jump.

1908—Invents new trick, the Water Can Escape.

1909—Returns to Europe; Learns to fly an airplane while performing in Germany.

1910—Performs in Australia and is the first to fly an airplane in that country on March 16.

1912—Invents the Water Torture Cell Escape, which he first performs in Germany.

1913—Cecilia Weiss dies of a stroke; Houdini is stricken with grief.

1914—Performs trick called Walking Through a Brick Wall.

1915—First performs straitjacket escapes while hanging from skyscrapers.

1918—First performs the Vanishing Elephant trick; Acts in a silent serial movie called *The Master Mystery*.

1919—Stars in *The Grim Game* and *Terror Island*.

1920—Meets author and spiritualist Sir Arthur Conan Doyle while performing in England; Attends séances in an attempt to contact his mother's spirit.

1922—Stars in *The Man From Beyond*; Fails to reach his mother during a special séance with the Doyles; Begins to attack spiritualism; Stars in *Haldane of the Secret Service*.

1924—Lectures on fake mediums; Attends séances given by medium Mina Crandon and exposes her tricks.

1926—Survives in sealed coffin underwater for one and a half hours; Is punched in the stomach by a college student in Montreal, Canada, on October 22; Ruptured appendix is removed during emergency surgery in Detroit, Michigan, on October 25; Dies of resulting infection on October 31, Halloween; Is buried at Machpelah Cemetery in Queens, New York.

1943—Bess Houdini dies of a heart attack.

CHAPTER NOTES

Chapter 1. Showman and Mythmaker

1. Kenneth Silverman, *Houdini!!! The Career of Ehrich Weiss* (New York: HarperCollins Publishers, Inc., 1996), p. 31.

2. William Lindsay Gresham, *Houdini: The Man Who Walked Through Walls* (New York: Henry Holt and Co., 1959), p. 141.

3. Ruth Brandon, *The Life and Many Deaths of Harry Houdini* (New York: Random House, 1993), p. 131.

4. Doug Henning, *Houdini: His Legend and His Magic* (New York: Times Books, 1977), p. 70.

Chapter 2. Ehrich Weiss Becomes Harry Houdini

1. Ruth Brandon, *The Life and Many Deaths of Harry Houdini* (New York: Random House, 1993), p. 24.

2. Ibid., p. 25.

3. Doug Henning, *Houdini: His Legend and His Magic* (New York: Times Books, 1977), p. 25.

4. Brandon, pp. 21–22.

5. Ibid., p. 22.

6. Ibid., p. 115.

7. Ibid., p. 29.

8. Ibid.

9. Raymund Fitzsimons, *Death & The Magician: The Mystery of Houdini* (New York: Atheneum, 1981), p. 19.

10. William Lindsay Gresham, *Houdini: The Man Who Walked Through Walls* (New York: Henry Holt and Co., 1959), p. 26.

11. Brandon, p. 44.

12. Ibid., p. 50.

Chapter 3. Years of Struggle

1. William Lindsay Gresham, *Houdini: The Man Who Walked Through Walls* (New York: Henry Holt and Co., 1959), p. 28.

2. Raymund Fitzsimons, *Death & The Magician: The Mystery of Houdini* (New York: Atheneum, 1981), p. 22.

3. Ruth Brandon, *The Life and Many Deaths of Harry Houdini* (New York: Random House, 1993), p. 62.

4. Gresham, pp. 34–35.

5. Brandon, p. 65.

6. James C. Young, "Magic and Mediums," *The New York Times*, May 7, 1922, p. 2.

7. Gresham, p. 63.

8. Brandon, p. 82.

9. Milbourne Christopher, *Houdini: A Pictorial Life* (New York: Thomas Y. Crowell Company, 1976), p. 14.

10. Fitzsimons, p. 39.

11. Brandon, p. 78.

12. Fitzsimons, p. 38.

13. James Stewart-Gordon, "Houdini, the Man No Lock Could Hold," *The Reader's Digest*, February 1976, p. 154.

Chapter 4. Triumph in Europe

1. James Stewart-Gordon, "Houdini, the Man No Lock Could Hold," *The Reader's Digest*, February 1976, p. 154.

2. William Lindsay Gresham, *Houdini: The Man Who Walked Through Walls* (New York: Henry Holt and Co., 1959), pp. 82–83.

3. Kenneth Silverman, *Houdini!!! The Career of Ehrich Weiss* (New York: HarperCollins Publishers, Inc., 1996), p. 49.

4. Ruth Brandon, *The Life and Many Deaths of Harry Houdini* (New York: Random House, 1993), p. 90.

5. Ibid., p. 77.

6. Ibid., p. 92.

7. Silverman, p. 96.

8. Brandon, p. 95.

9. Stewart-Gordon, p. 152.

10. Brandon, p. 110.

11. Silverman, p. 59.

12. Gresham, p. 109.

13. Ibid., p. 110.

14. Brandon, p. 101.

15. Silverman, p. 268.

16. Brandon, pp. 137–138.

Chapter 5. Conquering New Challenges

1. Doug Henning, *Houdini: His Legend and His Magic* (New York: Times Books, 1977), p. 66.

2. Ruth Brandon, *The Life and Many Deaths of Harry Houdini* (New York: Random House, 1993), pp. 143–144.

3. William Lindsay Gresham, *Houdini: The Man Who Walked Through Walls* (New York: Henry Holt and Co., 1959), pp. 135–136.

4. Brandon, p. 74.

5. Ibid., p. 130.

6. Ibid., p. 145.

7. Ibid., p. 147.

8. Ibid., p. 158.

9. Milbourne Christopher, *Houdini: A Pictorial Life* (New York: Thomas Y. Crowell Company, 1976), p. 66.

10. Ibid., p. 71.

11. Ibid., p. 72.

12. Kenneth Silverman, *Houdini!!! The Career of Ehrich Weiss* (New York: HarperCollins Publishers, Inc., 1996), p. 143.

13. Brandon, p. 156.

14. Christopher, p. 78.

Chapter 6. Death-Defying Entertainer

1. Ruth Brandon, *The Life and Many Deaths of Harry Houdini* (New York: Random House, 1993), p. 27.

2. Kenneth Silverman, *Houdini!!! The Career of Ehrich Weiss* (New York: HarperCollins Publishers, Inc., 1996), p. 167.

3. Ibid., p. 164.

4. Ibid., p. 167.

5. Brandon, p. 170.

6. William Lindsay Gresham, *Houdini: The Man Who Walked Through Walls* (New York: Henry Holt and Co., 1959), p. 183.

7. Brandon, p. 174.

8. Silverman, p. 181.

9. Francis Sill Wickware, "Hairbreadth Harry Houdini," *The Reader's Digest*, March 1943, p. 64.

10. Ibid.

11. Silverman, p. 197.

12. Brandon, p. 190.

13. Milbourne Christopher, *Houdini: A Pictorial Life* (New York: Thomas Y. Crowell Company, 1976), p. 46.

14. Ibid.

15. Gresham, p. 201.

16. Brandon, p. 34.

17. Christopher, p. 156.

18. Ibid., p. 158.

19. Doug Henning, *Houdini: His Legend and His Magic* (New York: Times Books, 1977), p. 173.

Chapter 7. Movie Star

1. Ruth Brandon, *The Life and Many Deaths of Harry Houdini* (New York: Random House, 1993), p. 204.

2. Kenneth Silverman, *Houdini!!! The Career of Ehrich Weiss* (New York: HarperCollins Publishers, Inc., 1996), p. 239.

3. Brandon, p. 239.

4. Bernard M. L. Ernst, *Houdini and Conan Doyle* (New York: Benjamin Blom, Inc., 1972), p. 70.

5. Brandon, p. 240.

6. Ibid., p. 194.

7. Ibid.

8. Ibid., p. 251.

9. Ibid., p. 252.

10. Raymund Fitzsimons, *Death & The Magician: The Mystery of Houdini* (New York: Atheneum, 1981), p. 117.

11. Brandon, pp. 255–256.

12. Ibid., p. 257.

13. Ernst, p. 175.

Chapter 8. Crusader Against Spiritualist Frauds

1. Kenneth Silverman, *Houdini!!! The Career of Ehrich Weiss* (New York: HarperCollins Publishers, Inc., 1996), p. 298.

2. Ruth Brandon, *The Life and Many Deaths of Harry Houdini* (New York: Random House, 1993), p. 231.

3. Silverman, p. 306.

4. Brandon, p. 264.

5. Ibid., p. 268.

6. Ibid.

7. Ibid.

8. Raymund Fitzsimons, *Death & The Magician: The Mystery of Houdini* (New York: Atheneum, 1981), p. 139.

9. Brandon, p. 267.

10. Fitzsimons, p. 141.

11. "Houdini Assails Medium as Fraud," *The New York Times*, December 20, 1924, p. 18.

12. "Houdini Wins Test in a Sealed Coffin," *The New York Times*, August 6, 1926, p. 32.

Chapter 9. The Final Performance

1. James Stewart-Gordon, "Houdini, the Man No Lock Could Hold," *The Reader's Digest*, February 1976, p. 155.

2. Ruth Brandon, *The Life and Many Deaths of Harry Houdini* (New York: Random House, 1993), p. 288.

3. Milbourne Christopher, *The Illustrated History of Magic* (New York: Thomas Y. Crowell Company, 1973), p. 364.

4. Brandon, p. 290.

5. Ibid., p. 291.

6. William Lindsay Gresham, *Houdini: The Man Who Walked Through Walls* (New York: Henry Holt and Co., 1959), pp. 285–286.

7. Ibid., p. 286.

8. Brandon, p. 298.

9. Gresham, p. 297.

10. *Time*, November 9, 1936, p. 48.

11. Bernard M. L. Ernst, *Houdini and Conan Doyle* (New York: Benjamin Blom, Inc., 1972), p. 16.

12. Edmund Wilson, "A Great Magician," *The New Republic*, October 17, 1928, p. 250.

13. Kenneth Silverman, *Houdini!!! The Career of Ehrich Weiss* (New York: HarperCollins Publishers, Inc., 1996), p. 203.

14. Brandon, p. 55.

GLOSSARY

acute—Severe; serious; demanding immediate attention.

animation—The act of putting into motion or giving life.

apparatus—Materials or equipment designed for a particular use.

appendicitis—An inflammation of the appendix, which is a tube-shaped sac attached to the large intestine.

apprentice—One who is learning a trade or art from someone more experienced.

burlap—A coarse, heavy woven fabric.

cannibal—A person who eats human flesh.

circuit—A number or series of public outlets (in this case, theaters).

climax—The point of highest dramatic tension.

colossal—Enormous or incredible.

conjurer—One who practices magic arts.

crusade—An enterprise undertaken with energy and enthusiasm.

dialect—A regional variety of language.

fatal—Resulting in death.

goatee—A small beard on a man's chin.

inauguration—A ceremony for swearing a person into office.

lecture—An instructive talk given to an audience.

lunatic asylum—A hospital for insane people.

manacle—A shackle for a hand, wrist, or leg; a restraint.

matinee—An afternoon performance.

megaphone—A cone-shaped device open at both ends and used to make the voice louder and send it in a certain direction.

moor—To hold in place with rope, cable, or anchor.

pallbearer—A person who helps to carry the coffin at a funeral.

parallel—Similar or matching; at an equal distance side by side.

phenomena—Rare or significant facts or events.

pier—A structure extending into water for use as a landing place; dock.

pillar—An upright support or post.

precinct—A division of a city for police control.

publicity—A stunt or advertisement designed to attract public interest.

rabbi—A Jewish religious leader.

rivet—A metal pin or bolt used to fasten two pieces of metal.

serial—A series or number of episodes.

skewer—A large pin for fastening meat while cooking.

skyscraper—A very tall building.

slander—A false charge or statement.

span—To extend across.

surgeon—A doctor who specializes in diseases and cures that require operations.

tambourine—A small, shallow drum with disks at the sides played by shaking, striking, or rubbing.

testify—To make a statement under oath.

truant—One who stays away without permission.

zinc—A metallic element often used as a protective coating for iron or steel.

FURTHER READING

Books

Cox, Clinton. *Houdini.* New York: Scholastic Inc., 2001.

Lalicki, Tom. *Spellbinder: The Life of Harry Houdini.* New York: Holiday House Inc., 2000.

Rau, Dana Meachen. *Harry Houdini: Master Magician.* Danbury, Conn.: Franklin Watts Inc., 2001.

Sabin, Louis. *The Great Houdini: Daring Escape Artist.* Mahwah, N.J.: Troll Communications, 1999.

Woog, Adam. *Harry Houdini.* San Diego, Calif.: Lucent Books, 1995.

Internet Addresses

Hargrave. "Harry Houdini: aviation pioneer (1874–1926)." *The Pioneers: Saluting the Men & Women of Aviation History.* January 5, 2002. <http://www.ctie.monash.edu.au/hargrave/houdini_bio.html>.

"Houdini Historical Center." n.d. <http://www.foxvalleyhistory.org/houdini/>.

Joan F. Higbee. "Houdini: A Bibliographical Chronology." *Library of Congress.* October 1996. <http://lcweb2.loc.gov/ammem/vshtml/vshchrn.html>.

INDEX